Morality and Youth

Morality and Youth
A GUIDE
FOR CHRISTIAN PARENTS

By
F. Philip Rice

THE WESTMINSTER PRESS
PHILADELPHIA

BOOK DESIGN BY DOROTHY ALDEN SMITH

First edition

Published by The Westminster Press ®
Philadelphia, Pennsylvania

PRINTED IN THE UNITED STATES OF AMERICA
9 8 7 6 5 4 3 2 1

Library of Congress Cataloging in Publication Data

Rice, F   Phillip.
  Morality and Youth.

  Bibliography: p.
  1. Youth—Conduct of life. 2. Moral education.
3. Christian ethics—United Church of Christ authors.
I. Title.
BJ1661.R5   241   80–11433
ISBN 0–664–24315–0

To Irma

whose love and basic goodness
transcends all space and time
and will be felt for generations to come

Contents

Preface

Since I spend much of my time writing, friends and family members ask quite frequently: "What book are you working on now?" During recent months, my answer has been: "I'm writing a book on Morality and Youth." This reply has been greeted with incredulous stares: "Morality and youth! I didn't know there was any morality among our youth."

This attitude reflects a widespread feeling among adults that our young people aren't as moral as they should be. But when some adults think of morality, they refer only to sexual morality, or immorality, as the case may be. But this is only part of the total picture. It's misleading to generalize about the morality of today's youths, since there is such a wide variation among them. Surveys actually reveal little straying from orthodoxy, deep religious concerns, and much youthful idealism among a significant minority of young people. Many other youths show deep social concern, an antimaterialistic ethic, an emphasis on preserving family values, love, openness, and trust. Premarital sexual behavior has changed very rapidly, and I have attempted to analyze and discuss this from a Christian perspective.

But the important emphasis in this book is not on the degree of morality or immorality which adults feel exists

among youths, but on the *process* by which moral character and behavior are developed. One of the major purposes in writing this book is to try to fill this void: to discuss
how Christian character and morals are formed and to
emphasize the various methods of moral teaching and the
roles of the family, peer groups, television and movies, the
schools, and the churches in the process. It is my hope that
by understanding the process of moral development from
a child-development and Christian education perspective,
parents, teachers, youth leaders, pastors, and other thinking adults will be able to exert a more vital influence over
the process.

A second major purpose of the book is to provide some
of the *content* of this moral teaching. With this purpose in
mind, five different areas of ethical decision-making have
been chosen for discussion. These five areas are: choosing
a vocation, marriage and family values, sexual attitudes
and behavior, drug abuse, and juvenile crime and delinquency. Numerous other areas might have been included,
but these topics have been selected because of widespread
concern about them.

I have also tried to write a book that is thoroughly Christian. I feel it is both unwise and almost impossible to remain morally neutral in any discussion of morality. For this
reason, I have no hesitancy in acknowledging that an overall goal is to stimulate readers to search for truth as revealed by God in Christ, and to direct them in their efforts
to teach the Christian faith and ethic to young people.
While I try to avoid dogmatism in an educational book,
and to approach each question and problem with an honest mind, my value stance throughout is the Christian faith
and the teachings of Christ.

I do feel that the Christian ethic without the Christian
faith is difficult, and that ultimately youths become moral

when they are committed to a cause, an idea, a person, a God. Modern young people have shown just as much willingness to commit themselves as ever before, but that commitment is sometimes to "other Gods," other faiths, other causes. The challenge to Christian adults is to ask for uncompromising commitment to Christ.

F.P.R.

Part I
THE MORAL REALM

1
Religion, Morality, and Today's Youths

Adults of every generation tend to feel that their young people are less moral than were those of previous generations.

> Our earth is degenerate these days; there are signs that the world is speedily coming to an end; bribery and corruption are common; children no longer obey their parents; and the end of the world is evidently approaching.

This message was carved on an Assyrian stone tablet that dates from 2800 B.C.! But a similar feeling was expressed forty-seven centuries later, in 1921, in the *Century Magazine:*

> It seems that young people have taken the bit between their teeth and are running wild. They are wholly contemptuous of the traditional controls. . . . Fond parents, maiden aunts, all the amateur censors of morals are at their wits' end . . . and the end is not in sight. . . .
> The elders of today are convinced that no age . . . has had on its hands such a problem of reckless and rebellious youth. (Donovan, 1967, p. 192)

It is easy to be critical of the behavior of adolescents. Adults were young once, but they have conveniently forgotten how mischievous they were and how much worry they caused their parents. Or, adults remember the trouble *they* got into, so they project their own fears and anxieties onto their teenagers and criticize them partly out of fear that they will get into trouble too. If we are to evaluate the moral growth and development of adolescents, there is a need to take a more objective look at today's youths, to discover their moral strengths and their weaknesses.

AN AGE OF IDEALISM

Adolescents are both highly critical of adults and quite idealistic in their views of the world. Recently, a young person commented:

> As far as I can see, adults have pretty much made a mess of the world. The environment is polluted, our energy resources are exhausted, our cities are centers of crime, the country is on the verge of bankruptcy, marriages are breaking up everywhere, the churches are ineffective, politicians are corrupt, and education is a farce. And then they have the nerve to say that we're immoral!

This type of criticism is characteristic of young people of every generation. One college student during the Roaring Twenties commented:

> I would like to observe that the older generation had pretty much ruined this world before passing it on to us. They give us this Thing, knocked to pieces, leaky, red-hot, threatening to blow up, and then they are surprised that we don't accept it with the same attitude of pretty, decorous enthusiasm with which they received it, 'way back in the eighteen-nineties, nicely painted, smoothly running, practically foolproof. (Donovan, 1967, p. 1965)

There are several reasons why children become very critical when they reach adolescence. One important reason is that they develop the ability to reason abstractly. They are able to think beyond the concrete present, able to think about what isn't yet, about what might be possible. This growing ability to distinguish the possible from the real enables them to discern not only what the adult world is but what it might be like under the most ideal circumstances (Rice, 1978, p. 561). This ability is what makes them idealistic rebels. They set themselves up as critical observers of things as they are, and they become ultracritical of adults as well.

Another reason adolescents become critical is that their own self-consciousness is growing. As they develop the capacity to think about their own thoughts, they become sensitively aware of themselves, their persons and ideas. As a result, they become very egocentric, self-conscious, and introspective. They develop the feeling that they are on stage much of the time, that others are as concerned with them as they are. Consequently, much of their time is spent "reacting to an imaginary audience" (Elkind, 1967, p. 1030). One result is that they become critical and sarcastic in their relationship to others—partly as a defense against their own feelings of inferiority, and partly as a way of making themselves look good.

While adolescents are self-conscious, they are also self-admiring and egocentric. Some develop the equivalent of a messiah complex. In all modesty they attribute to themselves essential roles in the salvation of the world. They may make a pact with God, promising to serve him without return, but planning to play a decisive role in the cause they espouse (Piaget, 1967). They see themselves in a major effort to reform the world, and they are quite critical of adults who do not share their views and who have not already become reformers also. As they become aware of their newly acquired intellectual capacities, they devote themselves in excited exchange with like-minded friends to the criticism of the older generation and of current institutions in the search for a more just society (Adelson, 1972, p. 120).

Because of their own inner turmoil, most adolescents have an empathetic capacity to understand the sufferings of others. Because of their own insecurities, they can identify with the weak, the poor, the oppressed, the victims of a selfish society. Social injustices remind them of their own individual, internal struggles for equality (Rice, 1978, p. 562).

Young adolescents express their idealistic rebellion primarily on a verbal level. They will complain loudly, but are not able to channel their energies into long-term, constructive projects and causes. Junior highs, for example, will show much enthusiasm about problems of the elderly, but after only one effort will not show up when subsequent opportunities are provided to help. Their enthusiasm is easily stimulated, but just as quickly subsides. This is quite typical of immature persons. They would rather complain about the problems of the world than do something about them.

Older adolescents are more likely to become activists. They may become caught up in political protests and reform movements of various kinds, or in long-term service projects such as the Peace Corps. They will join fanatical religious movements that promise to save individual souls or evangelize the world. Once they discover possible courses of action, they pour themselves into these endeavors, into ideation, fantasy, and the building of brave new doctrines and worlds.

Youth is a time for dreaming. Youths can solve any problem in the world. They can indulge in wild flights of imagination, soaring speculations, and incredible adventures;

their fantasies know no limits. Only little by little do they discover that there may be limits to reality and that it is harder to solve world problems than it is to think about them. If given the right chance and motivation, however, their idealistic energies can be channeled into constructive, positive actions (Oates, 1969, p. 105).

A TIME FOR EXAMINATION

Up until adolescence, children have pretty much accepted, uncritically, the moral values they have been taught. If their parents have been fairly close to them, and if their parents are the type of people they can admire and respect, they have modeled much of their behavior after them and are fond of quoting what their parents have said when talking to friends.

But at adolescence, this picture slowly changes. Youths begin to examine traditional teachings and values in which they were brought up. Their courses in school, their broadening contacts with an increasing circle of friends, their exposure to other religions and values through reading and television and other forms of mass media, all stimulate their thinking about their own values. The more adolescents mature intellectually, and the more they are exposed to mental stimulation, the more they begin to question, to doubt, and to challenge the values in which they were reared. Thus, broadening social and educational experiences result in a more reasoned and less authoritarian interpretation of religion and ethics. Adolescents' views become more liberal, more tolerant, and less dogmatic (Rice, 1978, p. 491).

This is as it should be, because persons do not really become moral until they are free to choose between good and evil, and then voluntarily decide to choose the good

(Pomeroy, 1974, p. 249). Those who have no choice and do the right are amoral rather than moral. Their morality is not theirs; it has been given by parents or forced by those in authority. They have not accepted, internalized, or practiced it of their own free will in the sense that they believe in it and want to follow it. There are some youths like this. Their religion is still that of their parents, and not of their own choosing. An unexamined faith or untested values are the first to be weakened when challenged by contrary beliefs or ethics.

Adolescence is a time for rebellion against external authority, including the religious domination of parents. Young people need a chance to question what they have always been taught as true. And most important, they need a chance to decide their own faith and values for themselves.

This whole idea makes some parents panicky. They are afraid their teenagers will reject everything they have been taught, or adopt values that will get them into trouble. So such parents try to hold on even tighter. This stimulates the youths who have more rebellious natures to repudiate "the faith of their fathers" and the more timid ones to conform obediently without real understanding. Either extreme results in a lower level of spiritual maturity. For this reason parents need to be willing to discuss any and all religious questions, to encourage their young people to examine critically their own values, and to be willing to explain why they, as religious adults, think as they do. Parents who have strong beliefs *should* defend them, to the best of their ability, but should not expect blind acceptance or agreement without thought. Sometimes adolescents will argue vehemently, and it seems that they haven't listened or accepted one word that has been taught, but they will subsequently quote the same ideas to their friends as though they were their own truths. Even if these youths do reject their parents' values, the parents will have done a good job because they have helped their young people to think about what values they can hold for themselves.

TRADITION AND CHANGE

Young people tend to be critical of tradition. Because they see themselves as the "mod" generation, they tend to look upon anything old as outdated, old-fashioned, and hence unusable. When Dad recalls "how things were when I was growing up," the adolescent responds, "But, Dad, it's not like that anymore." As a result, the two generations have trouble understanding and communicating with each other. The more adolescents feel their parents' ideas are old-fashioned and reject their ideas, the more difficult it is for parents to exercise influence, and the more likely that conflict and misunderstanding will result. One of the most common complaints of parents today is that their teenagers don't seem to listen to anything they have to say.

Most parents will be glad to know that many of their teachings do *not* fall on deaf ears. A national study of youths, ages 16 to 25, found that two out of three believed that extramarital sexual relationships were wrong, as were taking things without paying for them and destroying private property (Yankelovich, 1974, pp. 67, 93). Almost 90 percent held that love and friendship were very important personal values. There had been an increase (to about 60 percent) in the proportion of youths who believed that doing things for others was a very important value (p. 93). About three out of four felt that there should be less emphasis on money in our society (p. 93). Certainly this does not add up to an antichristian ethic or promise mass rejection of traditional parental values.

However, some values are changing. This same national study revealed that a decreasing proportion of college youths (38 percent) and noncollege youths (45 percent) felt they could willingly and easily accept prohibitions against marijuana. Only 22 percent of college youths and 34 percent of noncollege youths felt that casual premarital sexual relations were wrong. Also a decreasing proportion of college youths (32 percent) and noncollege youths (48 percent) thought having an abortion was wrong (Yankelovich, 1974, pp. 93, 94).

What is happening is that youths are rejecting traditional values in certain areas (premarital sex and marijuana use being the most noticeable), causing some adults to exclaim that today's youths are immoral. Only a small percentage of adults, for example, have tried marijuana, whereas a majority of college-age youths have. This wide difference between the practices of adults and youths indicates that young people are rejecting their parental values with regard to this practice. The same is true with regard to sexual attitudes; youths are considerably more liberal than adults (Rice, 1978, p. 286).

But in other areas youth are manifesting improved morality. Certainly the decline of interest in materialism and the renewed emphasis on humanistic values would indicate a superior moral code according to traditional Judeo-Christian ethics. One cannot say, therefore, that all young people are moral (or immoral), or that all reject (or accept) traditional values. It depends upon what values you are talking about.

There are wide differences, also, among different groups of adolescents. Parental influence is greatest at the sixth-grade level and declines thereafter (Floyd and South,

1972). College freshmen show less disagreement with parents on certain social problems than do college juniors and seniors. College-educated youths tend to disagree with parents more often than noncollege young people. Apparently, increases in age and education widen the gap between parents and adolescents. Also, males tend to show more disagreement with parents than do females (Jacobsen, 1975). It is both unwise and inaccurate, therefore, to try to categorize all youths today as either moral or immoral. Some are moral and some are not. The differences among young people are as great as the differences within other age groups in the population. Stereotyping of any group is to be avoided.

CHURCH AND ORTHODOXY

There does seem to be some evidence that decreasing numbers of youths are participating in the institutionalized church. One survey of adolescents in grades 10 to 12 in a southern community showed that from 1964 to 1974 church attendance of both black and white males decreased significantly. Attendance of both black and white females, however, increased slightly over the decade (Dickinson, 1976). See Figure 1-1. Both males and females showed a decline in frequency of Bible-reading and in saying grace at mealtimes. Whites continued to be more avid Bible readers than blacks, but more blacks said grace at meals. The important point is that there was a decline in frequency of participation in these religious activities (Dickinson, 1976).

The same holds true for college-age youths. Surveys of Williams College men from 1948 to 1974 showed an increasing percentage rejecting the religious group in which they were brought up, and, in general, disengaging them-

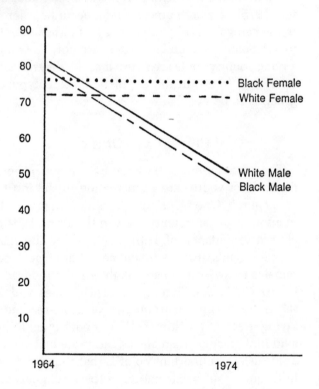

Figure 1-1

FREQUENCY OF CHURCH ATTENDANCE
OF HIGH SCHOOL YOUTHS
IN A SOUTHERN COMMUNITY, 1964-1974

Percent Attending Church
Once a Week or More

From G. E. Dickinson, "Religious Practices of Adolescents in a Southern Community: 1964-1974," *Journal for the Scientific Study of Religion* 15 (Dec. 1976): 361-363. Used by permission of the Society for the Scientific Study of Religion, Inc., and G. E. Dickinson.

selves from the church (Hastings and Hoge, 1976). According to the 1974 survey, 83 percent of the students were reared Catholic, Orthodox, Protestant, or Jewish, but only 26 percent said these traditions were adequate for them. Many of the Catholic or Protestant students who shifted their religious preferences felt that a more liberalized, ethical type of Christianity was preferable to the traditional type in which they were brought up. Other students dropped all expressions of religion, while others turned to new forms such as those found in the Eastern religions or in highly evangelistic sects of the Pentecostal type. Overall, there was a decline in the percentage of students who prayed or who experienced feelings of reverence or devotion toward a Supreme Being.

What about religious beliefs? Although there was some weakening of belief in traditional Judeo-Christian doctrines from 1948 to 1967, there was relatively little change after that. In 1974, a full 60 percent of the students reported that they required some form of religious orientation or belief in order to achieve a fully mature philosophy of life (Hastings and Hoge, 1976, p. 242). Seventy-nine percent of the students reported that there had been a period in their lives when they had reacted either partially or wholly against the beliefs they had been taught, but a full 70 percent were still in partial agreement with those beliefs, 10 percent were in full agreement, and only 21 percent wholly disagreed with them (Hastings and Hoge, 1976, p. 247). The picture we get is one of students reacting against the institutionalized church, continuing to hold on to many of their religious beliefs, but experimenting with numerous substitute forms of religious expression.

Opportunity for Commitment

At the same time that many youths are disengaging themselves from the organized church, they are searching for substitute causes to which they can give their allegiance. Youth are in the process of finding their identity, of answering the age-old questions: Who am I? Why am I here? What do I seek? What do I want to do with my life? Many youths are finding their identities by allying themselves with a cause or group to which they can give wholehearted allegiance. The success of such groups as the "Jesus movement" or the "Moonies" in winning thousands of young people to their causes is proof positive that youths can be reached if sufficiently challenged. But the primary appeal of such groups is that they ask for complete commitment, not just for an hour or so of attention each week. "When you join their church, you join full time and commit your whole life" (Sontag, 1977, p. 271). It is no accident that the fastest growing religious groups today, such as the Mormons or the highly evangelistic sects, are those which emphasize the greatest involvement and participation of their members in the ongoing ministry of the church. It seems that the more churches demand of their members in the way of personal participation and sacrifice, the greater their appeal to youths who need causes in which to invest their lives. Many young persons have found meaning in groups like the Peace Corps, or in political activist or protest movements. But countless thousands are also answering the appeal of Christ to "follow me." The challenge to parents and other adults is to so teach Christ, and to ask for total commitment to him, that youths will find meaningful and moral living through serving him.

This commitment can come in a variety of ways. For some, it comes through a conversion experience. Babin (1962) writes:

> The central point toward which the faith of adolescents is evolving is a crisis, a conversion, which normally takes place between 17 and 25 years. It is important to be aware of this privileged moment, of this climax toward which adolescence is tending. (P. 128)

Babin emphasizes that this conversion is not always highly dramatic, but it always involves a crisis of commitment (Babin, 1969). "In every case, the faith of adolescents takes on meaning only in relation to this point of crisis and resolution" (Babin, 1962, p. 129).

In some instances, of course, the conversion *is* dramatic. The evangelical groups emphasize the need to be saved, to be reborn, so their efforts are bent on getting the young person involved in a drastic, stressful, emotional experience. One student recalls:

> While I was home, my brother, who had been a Christian for about six months, occasionally took me to some meetings conducted by a group called Young Life. I went basically because I felt close to my brother and wanted to see what he was into. . . .
>
> They started talking about a relationship with Jesus . . . and afterward they gave an invitation to anybody to come up and rap with them. Even though I normally would have passed it up because my mind was made up about God, something took me up there to talk to Phil the drummer.
>
> "Ask Jesus into your life," he said, "and be willing to follow Him. He will let you know that He is there." . . .
>
> Finally that night in bed I said, "Jesus, come into my life. I'll believe you if you show me that you are there and that you are real." . . .
>
> He had to show me if He was real. And He **did**. All those

things I had been into before vanished and suddenly seemed absurd. . . .

Now love is something that can be lived and not just talked about. Where all the philosophy, drugs, and revolutionary doctrine had been, Jesus now lives and works and protects and guides my living. Now I know that He has planned and is enacting the greatest possible life I could have. (Curtis, 1971)

Those churches which are more liberal emphasize that religious consciousness during adolescence ought to be a continuation of the gradual religious awakening begun during childhood. Faith is examined, refined, and strengthened, but not radically changed.

Children reared with love and faith, taught over a period of years, don't need to be converted in a sudden, dramatic way, because they are already Christians. Only those reared apart from the faith with different values and separated from the love of God need be saved. Conversion implies change, but why wait until adolescence to accomplish the change? Why not nurture children as Christians from the time of their births, then change will not be necessary? . . . Why pray for the sudden salvation of children, but in the meantime, rear them in an atmosphere of unchristian love? (Rice, 1978, p. 489)

Whether conversion is catastrophic or gradual depends upon many factors. Certainly adolescents with unstable emotional temperaments, plagued by guilt and conflict, are predisposed to a dramatic type of religious experience, as are those reared in denominational groups emphasizing catastrophic religious conversion. Educated youths belonging to more formal churches are more likely to experience a gradual awakening.

All such youths need the opportunity to express their religious convictions through committed action. They can find their identity by enlisting in causes to which they can give themselves. Babin insists that the quest for identity expresses itself in the need to be recognized, accepted, and affirmed by others. With this desire comes a quest for participation that

> means placing one's own tiny block into the building of the world or into the highway of history, a stone that is small, but nonetheless necessary and important. Any expression— belonging to a union, supporting a family, working in a political campaign, participation in a movement—can be seen as a contribution to the improvement of society. It is clear that through this expression of self, this creation and this sharing, man finds an inherent meaning in life. (Babin, 1969, p. 33)

2
Measures and Meaning of Morality

According to the dictionary, to be moral means "conforming to the rules of right conduct, following generally accepted customs of conduct and right living in society." But the important question is: whose rules, whose standards, and which society are you talking about? Today's youths are confused because they live in a society that emphasizes not one standard but many. Ours is a pluralistic culture in which various value systems and standards of conduct exist side by side, each accepted or practiced by some group or person. The result is confusion. Youths ask: "How can you tell right from wrong? Who is to decide? Isn't it up to the individual person?" Or they say: "No one can decide for anyone else. It's up to the individual."

Part of the moral dilemma of today's youths arises as a crisis of authority. In the Temple, the chief priests and the elders asked Jesus, "By what authority are you doing these things and who gave you this authority?" (Matt. 21:23). Young people today are asking the same questions: "By what authority? By whose standards? Who says so?" There is a need, therefore, to take a look at various standards by which moral conduct is being judged before discussing the present situation in more detail.

INDIVIDUAL NORMS

Do Your Own Thing

A college student remarked:

> I think every person ought to be allowed to do his own thing. No one has any right to tell anyone else what to do. If I want to ride on my motorcycle without my helmet, and risk getting killed in an accident, who's to say I shouldn't be allowed to do it? It's my life, why should I have to do what anyone else says I should do?

Most of us have heard this same sentiment echoed over and over again in one form or another. Here are some other expressions of the same idea.

> *Teenage daughter to mother:* I don't see why I have to clean my room. It's my room, and I ought to be allowed to do with it exactly as I please. Why don't you just shut the door so you can't see the mess?
>
> *College son to father:* I'm not interested in spending my entire life making money. Just because you worked all your life doesn't mean I should. If I want to go through life being a bum, I think that's a decision which only I can make. I've decided that I don't want to go to work right now. I'd like to travel around the country first, and find out what life is all about.
>
> *Adolescent to friend:* I think Joan is foolish, but if she wants to sleep with as many boys as she can, that's up to her. I don't feel I have any right to tell her what to do.

Most thoughtful youths will qualify the "do your own thing" ethic by adding that it's all right "as long as you don't hurt anyone else." This represents some acknowledgment that one person does not have the right to infringe upon the rights of others. But my own reaction to the "do your own thing" philosophy as presently practiced by today's youths is that it overlooks the extent to which each person is dependent upon many others, and it minimizes the effect that one person's behavior has upon others. Adolescents like to feel that they are independent because it makes them feel they are grown up. But no one is completely independent. All of us need someone, and since we do, other lives are affected by the way we live. Consider the following examples:

> Kate felt that the decision to smoke pot was her business, and no one else's. But while stoned, she became involved in a bad auto accident and totaled her car. Her parents had to pay all her medical bills, and she injured two other people in the other vehicle.
>
> Bee felt that it was nobody's business whether she slept with her steady or not, but when she became pregnant, she asked her parents to pay for her abortion.

I am constantly amazed at the naiveté with which youths view their own actions as not affecting anyone else. Yet in actuality everything they do has some relationship to other persons. Even personal feelings and thoughts affect not only the individual but how that person acts in relationship to others. For example, whether I *feel* hostile —or loving—determines how I'm likely to act in personal encounters. Even if I commit so-called "victimless crimes," such as drinking myself to death, I have saddened the lives of all those who love me and care about me. There is no such thing as personal conduct that does not at some time affect someone else. The high school boy who drops out of school "to do his own thing" may hurt his parents if he has disappointed them.

There is one positive aspect about an individual standard of behavior. It does emphasize that each person is responsible. Ultimately, making moral choices is an individual matter even though the standard for choosing is not always individual. Each person must make a choice and then be willing to assume personal responsibility for the consequences. The young person who insists on choosing and then blames his or her parents when things go wrong has not yet become a moral adult. Morality involves making choices and accepting consequences.

Personal Adjustment

For years, psychologists and psychiatrists have emphasized that the right thing to do is what benefits the individual. If a particular action contributes to a person's mental health, happiness, sense of well-being, personality integration, and personal adjustment, then it is the right thing to do. If a specific action creates anxiety, conflict, insecurity, sadness, depression, or discontent and maladjustment, then it is bad for that person and ought not to be done. The acceptable standard of conduct, according to this view, is the overall effect upon the individual concerned.

This standard of behavior has often been applied to making decisions about sexual conduct. When youths ask, "Is it right or wrong to have premarital sexual intercourse?" the answer according to the standard of personal adjustment would be: "It depends. How do you feel about it? How do you react afterward? Has it helped you or harmed you? Has it made you a happier, more contented person, or has it resulted in guilt, anxiety, and conflict?"

While individuals must take into account the effect of their behavior on themselves, moral living does not always result in the maximum amount of personal happiness, or in a minimum of conflict and upset. Christ was tortured and condemned to death because he chose the right in opposition to a corrupt ecclesiastical system. He could have "adjusted," and created little trouble, and never been harmed personally. He had inner peace because he knew he was doing the will of the Father, but he made a poor adjustment to society.

Intuitive Guides

What about one's own intuition? If people follow their inclinations, will they do the right thing? They will, says Christian theologian Paul Lehmann, to the extent that they are transformed human beings. According to Lehmann, people do what they are: their actions are but an expression of their humanity. But that humanity must be transformed into the divine image by God's saving action in Christ. Thus, says Lehmann, "doing the will of God is doing what I am" (1963, p. 159). According to this view, only a godly person can do Godlike actions.

We have all known people who always seem to do the right thing—mothers who know almost instinctively how best to deal with their children, friends who are so sensitive to the feelings of others that they understand completely how they feel. But this is not a gift with which people are born. It develops over the years through loving, sensitive interaction with others and after countless experiences. It is a product of loving relationships, and a lifetime of relationships. Few young people are able to manifest this same sensitivity and wisdom in their dealings with others. Most youths chide themselves for their clumsy inability to relate to others in as sensitive a way as they themselves desire. This is why some Christian writers emphasize the need for a rational basis for moral actions, the need to use reason and the intellect in making moral judgments, since intuition alone is not a trustworthy guide (Wogaman, 1976, pp. 21–31).

An extreme case is represented by those persons who have become so hardened and insensitive that they can do almost anything and not feel guilty afterward. True, this is the abnormal person, the psychopathic personality without conscience. But because some persons have become this way, personal reactions alone cannot be considered an authoritative guide to moral conduct. People can get used to habitual wrongdoing. A young person who lies all the time can become so accustomed to lying that he or she no longer feels guilty or disturbed at all. When this point is reached, the conscience has ceased to function as an effective moral guide.

SOCIAL STANDARDS

Group Morality

This concept would emphasize that the standards of right conduct are determined not by individuals but by groups. Not only do young people say, "It's up to each individual," they also say, "Everybody's doing it." The theory is that if everyone else does something, or if "they say so," then it must be all right and so "I ought to be allowed to do it too." This consensus of the group or community becomes *the* standard by which right conduct is judged.

But the real question is: Who is everybody? Who are "they" to whom youths refer? "Everybody" can mean a small circle of friends or a clique of which the adolescent is a part. If the group says it's all right to do certain things, then this becomes the standard of right conduct. Of course, if a particular group emphasizes moral values that are in direct opposition to those of the larger social order, these deviant standards may place individuals in direct conflict with their larger community. The following deviant values were found to be important among one group of adolescent male delinquents:

1. The ability to keep one's mouth shut
2. The ability to be hard and tough
3. The ability to find kicks
4. The ability to make a fast buck
5. The ability to outsmart others
6. The ability to make connections with a racket

(Lerman, 1968)

Obviously, boys who held these values would be conforming to their own group, but these standards would be unacceptable as standards of right conduct for society as a whole.

People often accept the values of their group as right, proper, or good, but reject the standards of other groups as wrong, improper, or bad. So the particular standards depend upon the reference group of which one is a part.

Group standards can be useful for individuals to consider in governing their own actions. However, they need to compare their group with other groups. They need to learn to reject standards that do not seem to accord with more universally accepted principles. The more limited the group and the more its principles run counter to those of others, the more its standards may be suspect. True, even a whole society can be wrong and can sanction immoral acts, but several societies are more likely to point to universal truths than is one narrow, ingrown group.

Legal Sanctions

Some group standards of behavior are incorporated in civil law and so have the benefit of legal sanction and enforcement. Thus, not only is stealing considered morally wrong and unacceptable by most group standards but it is also recognized as unlawful and as a punishable crime. According to this view, morality is determined by civil law, and laws are needed as deterrents against wrongdoing.

However, there are some acts, such as adultery, which are against the law and condemned by the majority of persons in a society, but which are seldom prosecuted by law officers. Legal prohibitions are useless in deterring these actions, primarily because the laws are not enforced. In such cases, individual consciences and moral standards become far more effective deterrents.

Sometimes laws prohibit actions that are accepted and practiced by large groups of people. Laws against drinking alcoholic beverages and smoking marijuana are two good examples. Because so many people wanted to drink, laws of prohibition were, in the long run, useless in preventing it. The same thing is happening with marijuana. Even the strict application of laws against simple possession have been useless in preventing more and more youths from using the drug. Sometimes social pressure, such as the pressure to make drinking legal, is strong enough to force the laws to be changed.

Occasionally, civil law dictates actions that groups of persons or individuals consider immoral. Thus, pacifist religious groups that have taken a stand against military service or conscription and that urge their members not to register for the draft are expecting their members to violate civil law because they subscribe to moral principles that take precedence. Religious persons are sometimes forced to use civil disobedience as a means of calling attention to laws that they feel are unjust and immoral. They realize that they will have to suffer the consequences, but they are willing to do so in an effort to get the laws changed. Such was the position of Martin Luther King when he wrote from the Birmingham jail:

I do not advocate evading or defying the law. . . . That would lead to anarchy. One who breaks an unjust law must do so openly, lovingly, and with a willingness to accept the penalty. An individual who breaks the law that conscience tells him is unjust, and willingly accepts the penalty of imprisonment in order to arouse the conscience of the community over its injustice is, in reality, expressing the highest respect for the law. (King, 1964, p. 86)

What can we say about the function of law in influencing moral living? It is obvious that morality cannot be legislated. People will defy the law if they feel it is wrong, or if they make up their minds not to obey for one reason or another. Neither can civil law alone define what is moral or immoral. But civil law can help, not by defining, but by enforcing what has already been decided. Certainly, youths should be taught to obey the law insofar as the law is a reflection of universal moral principles to which religious persons can subscribe. If the law is wrong, the religious person has the responsibility to work to change it.

Situation Ethics
According to this concept, morality is determined not by individuals, social groups, or laws, but by situations and the effect of circumstances on the many persons involved. Absolutist legal or religious standards are rejected as too inflexible. Thus, whereas a church might say that divorce and remarriage are sinful, situation ethics would reject such an absolutist standard and say that it depends upon the circumstances, the motives and reasons, and the total effects upon all persons in and outside the family. Situation ethics would say that very few things are right or wrong in and of themselves. Their rightness or wrongness depends upon how they are used. Thus, alcohol can destroy human life if abused, or contribute to good health when

used medicinally. Even telling the truth can be an immoral act if done hurtfully and spitefully in a spirit of hatred or revenge rather than with tact, concern, and love. Fletcher writes:

> In Christian situation ethics nothing is worth anything in and of itself. It gains or acquires value only because it happens to help persons (thus being good) or to hurt persons (thus being bad). (Fletcher, 1966, p. 59)

Situation ethics would also reject individualistic standards of behavior as too self-centered and self-serving. The individual has to consider the effect of any course of behavior not only upon himself or herself but also upon all other persons who might be involved. Thus, the only standard considered appropriate is the concept of love. Fletcher goes on to say:

> No law or principle or value is good as such—not life or truth or chastity or property or marriage or anything but love. *Only one thing is intrinsically good, namely, love: nothing else at all.* (Fletcher, 1966, p. 68)

The task of the individual in making decisions is to determine what is the loving thing to do. Reason can help. The collective wisdom of generations can be a resource to enlighten judgment. The reactions and the effects of one's actions upon others can be a corrective guide. Wogaman observes that if it is love's intention to serve our neighbor, it is a long step toward fulfilling the intention if we can know what our neighbor's objective needs are likely to be (Wogaman, 1976, p. 16).

Situation ethics avoids the pitfalls of a legalistic, rigid application of laws and rules to govern conduct. Its big disadvantage is that circumstances can become a rationale for doubtful conduct. One example is the 1841 shipwreck of the *William Brown,* in the aftermath of which a ship's officer ordered a number of men to be thrown out of a perilously overloaded longboat. These men were sacrificed so that the remainder, including women and children, could survive (Wogaman, 1976, p. 16). The real question is whether the circumstances justified the action taken. Situation ethics really does not say that the end justifies the means. It would not agree with President Nixon that "national security" justified breaking into the democratic headquarters at Watergate or that the desire to keep South Vietnam from communist rule justified the suffering imposed by U.S. involvement in that war. It does say that both ends and means ought to express love and benefit rather than hurt for the persons involved.

CHRISTIAN NORMS

God's Will

Essentially, most religions strive to lift morality above the human plane and to discover the divine will. They reject the notion that human beings are "the measure of all truth." People are finite in their knowledge and understanding. Furthermore, their sinfulness and rebellion prevent full understanding and commitment to the perfect good. Their hope, therefore, is submission to divine authority, which is able to enlighten the mind and the will and guide actions. In this sense, to be moral means to be obedient to God, as the Supreme Being is revealed and understood.

Christ

For the Christian, this revelation is most complete in the person of Jesus. Because Christ is the revelation of God's character and will, his person and teachings become the standards of moral living.

Note that there are two ways by which Christ offers moral standards for the Christian. One is the example of his personality and life. Thus the Christian is one who strives to be "Christlike." Whatever virtue one attempts to describe—concern for the world, sensitivity to the feelings of others, courage in the face of danger, patience, the ability to forgive, humility, or wisdom—Christ provides an example that the Christian can imitate. In him the Word becomes flesh. Concepts of love, mercy, and compassion become real because they are demonstrated by what he does. He revealed moral living by healing Peter's mother-in-law, by restoring sight to a blind beggar, by eating with sinners, and by being obedient to God even unto death.

The second way that Christ provides moral standards for the Christian is through his teachings found in the parables, the Sermon on the Mount, and other places. How often we hear people say: "I believe in living by the Golden Rule," or "This world would be a better place to live in if we all lived by the principles of the Sermon on the Mount" (Kee, 1957, p. 14). But Christ's teachings are not to be interpreted legalistically as a new set of rules or as a codified system of ethics to replace the laws of Moses. For one thing, his teachings do not cover every conceivable situation. How simple it would be if Jesus had given a set of rules, sufficiently complete to enable us to run down through the code until we came to the precept that applied, and presto! the decision would be ready-made (Kee, 1957, p. 15). For another thing, to follow rules without regard for persons would be to act contrary to everything that Jesus tried to teach. He was concerned not with rules but with people, with what was best for persons. This is why he taught that by loving God and one's neighbor one would fulfill all that was written in the law and the prophets. Thus, Jesus could heal the sick on the Sabbath or pick grain for his disciples to eat, contrary to the code of the Pharisees. In so doing he illustrated that serving persons is more important than keeping laws just for the sake of keeping rules. "The sabbath was made for man, not man for the sabbath" (Mark 2:27). Wherever Jesus gives specific teachings, they are illustrative of important principles he is trying to teach rather than rules that can be applied to every situation. Thus, he could tell his listeners to "turn the other cheek," meaning that they should not feel obliged to retaliate whenever wronged, or to return evil for evil. But if we take this as a command never to stand up for ourselves and never to protect ourselves from abuse, or as an injunction to let others walk all over us, we are legalistically misinterpreting an important concept. Civil rights leaders used passive resistance to awaken the consciences of their oppressors, but they continued to resist oppression and to protest, nonviolently, against being persecuted and treated unjustly. They won, not by quiet submission, but by nonviolent protest. The task of the Christian is to understand the principles that Jesus is trying to teach and to apply those principles to solving contemporary problems.

Jesus was concerned not just with overt behavior but with motives, intentions, and feelings. "For out of the heart come evil thoughts, murder, adultery, fornication, theft, false witness, slander" (Matt. 15:19). He was concerned, therefore, with inner transformations of character, with the inner cleansing of the person, rather than with superficial improvements in behavior. "Woe to you, scribes and Pharisees, hypocrites! for you are like whitewashed tombs, which outwardly appear beautiful, but within they are full of dead men's bones and all unclean-ness" (Matt. 23:27). The Christian faith, therefore, seeks an inner reformation of the individual. This is accomplished through faith in Christ as saving Lord, and through repentance and submission to him. The more complete one's commitment, the more Christ is able to complete his sanctifying work in one's life. A person becomes more Christlike as he or she allows Jesus to become established as Lord and Savior.

The Bible

For the Christian, God in Christ—the living Word—is the real authority, but the record of that Word is most completely set forth in the Holy Scriptures of the Old and New Testaments. The Word is revealed through the prophets of the Old Testament whose teachings are but a preparation for the living revelation—the "Word made flesh" (John 1:14; Heb. 1:1, 2). Prior to the formation of the canon of the New Testament, however, church leaders assumed an authoritative role in interpretation. As the canon was formed, various individuals and councils sought to clear up controversial points. Ultimately, tradition came to bear more weight than Scripture itself, with the church assuming the final authority (Cully, 1963, p. 43).

The Protestant Reformation was based on the return to Scripture as the sole basis of authority. The Bible was to be read by individual Christians under the guidance of the Holy Spirit. But because humans are finite, fallible, and sinful, their understanding of God's word may vary. What is taught is sometimes the interpretation of a particular church or sect. Also, church creeds, the decisions of church councils, the interpretations of church leaders, and the findings of Biblical scholars have all been influential in molding individual thought. This is inevitable, since a true understanding and application of the Bible to modern life demands a dynamic interpretation to keep pace with an ever-changing world.

The Church

Individual Christians have always depended on the church to help them decide moral questions. While this has been more often true of Roman Catholics because their church has played a highly authoritarian role, Protestants have also sought to develop a moral consensus and their churches have published formal declarations at regional and national levels. The collective judgment of concerned and educated Christians, formally determined, is certainly a far better guide to moral living than individual opinions superficially expressed. Therefore it is necessary for church members to study the pronouncements of their churches on moral issues and to carry on a dialogue with other persons who are also striving to learn of God's will for their own lives. This is one reason why the fellowship of the church, the saving community, is so vital. Christians can help one another to know and understand their Lord's will.

The role of the pastor is a crucial one, because he or she plays a vital role in interpreting the Word to the flock. Wogaman writes:

> The pastor has, in effect, been designated by the community to reflect deeply on the meaning of Christian faith and to speak clearly and honestly to them about its interpretations for their lives. The process by which the pastor was originally designated and trained for this form of leadership [is] . . . likely to be conducive to more insightful moral leadership than might be expected from a random sampling of individual Christians. It is not irrational, therefore, to suppose that Christians will receive from the pulpit a form of

moral leadership which is worthy of respect. (Wogaman, 1976, p. 160)

Parents and young people alike need to learn to turn to their pastor for guidance. Most pastors can be a tremendously helpful influence.

Tradition

What has passed for Biblical prescriptions and authoritative pronouncements sometimes amounts to nothing more than social customs and traditions that have been given authority through usage and acceptance. Attitudes toward beards, dancing, moviegoing, clothing styles, and other things, though expressed with intense moral fervor, may reflect little more than the mores of a particular group. It is up to individual Christians, therefore, to try to sort out laws of human origin from divine commandments in deciding on proper moral conduct.

CONCLUSIONS

There are various norms by which people determine right from wrong. These may be summarized as follows:

Individual standards

What the person wants to do
What helps the individual
What intuition tells the person is the right thing

Social standards

What the group says is right
What is legal
What the situation demands

Christian standards

God's will
Christ's example and teachings
The Bible
The church
Tradition

Actually, these various standards are not mutually exclusive. Moral persons must be willing to assume individual responsibility for their actions. They strive to do what helps them and others and to sensitize their consciences to be reliable guides to moral conduct. They recognize that different groups emphasize different standards and that what is moral cannot always be equated with what any one group accepts, or even with what is declared legal. Also the rightness or wrongness of an action may, at times, depend upon the particular situation and the net effects of that action upon all persons involved.

Christians believe that morality must be lifted above the human plane and reside in the divine will. Created beings were never meant to live apart from God, but must look to him as the measure of all truth. In fact, they need his active presence working in their lives in order to be able to do his will. For the Christian, truth and power are personified in Christ, the Word made flesh. Christ's life and teachings are the foundation upon which a system of ethical living is to be built. Commitment to him through faith and repentance enables Christ to work in the life of the individual. The record of God's self-revelation is to be found in the Scriptures of the Old and New Testaments, which are the Word of God and the authoritative guide to truth and life. The commandments of God are best summarized in the commandment to love. Christians also look to the church—to its creeds, pronouncements, and teachings, and to its leaders—for the help they need in applying

God's Word to their own lives. Sometimes, traditions grow up in the church which are not authentic moral teachings, so it remains for the individual Christian, under the guidance of God's Word and Spirit, to sort out truth from error in order that he or she may remain faithful to Christ.

Part II
METHODS OF MORAL TEACHING

3
The Process
of Moral Development

A concerned parent asked, "How can I be certain that my child will grow up to be a moral person?" Of course, no parent can be completely certain. But by developing some understanding of how moral growth takes place, parents can more intelligently contribute in a positive way to the whole process.

TRADITIONAL APPROACHES

Moralizing and Memorization

Traditionally, moral education consisted primarily of the inculcation of values, either directly or indirectly. Direct approaches included attempts at indoctrination through moralizing and memorization. Children were required to learn such sayings as:

"Honesty is the best policy."
"The early bird gets the worm."
"A drunkard shall not inherit the kingdom of God."
"Honor thy father and mother."

I remember that part of our Sunday school work when I was growing up was to memorize key sections of Scripture: the Ten Commandments, the Beatitudes, the

51

Twenty-third Psalm, even the entire Sermon on the Mount. In fact, our dear mother gave us five cents for every verse of Scripture we memorized. The fact that we didn't understand the meaning of some of what we learned, or that we didn't really know whether or not it would work for us, was of no consequence so long as we learned it—that was the main thing. Someday, we were told, we would appreciate it, understand it, and use it. Then we would be grateful because of what our mother and teachers required us to do.

Unlike some educators, I feel that such methods do have some value. I remember how our mother always taught us: "You are to tell the truth. Don't lie, no matter what." There were times when trying to follow this precept got me into trouble with friends, and sometimes even with Mother. I learned that telling the truth was virtuous, and not always rewarding. However, this is an important value, and it was impressed upon us by the word of mouth, and by the virtuous example of our parents. Similarly, I do feel that memorizing the Ten Commandments and the Golden Rule had some value. They became definite guides to live by, particularly when explained and applied in specific ways to real-life situations.

I would agree with educators who emphasize that just telling children something doesn't mean they will do it. Certainly rote memorization without developing understanding is almost worthless in changing behavior. And I must admit that I was probably influenced more by the fine example of our parents than I was by what they said. I had a Sunday school teacher who supervised our memory work, but when we talked out of turn he whacked us over the head with the teacher's quarterly. I wouldn't have done anything he said.

Bag of Virtues Approach

Teaching prescribed moral virtues through moralization and indoctrination has been called the "bag of virtues" approach (Forisha and Forisha, 1976, p. 17). It has been a standard approach for generations. Aristotle proposed a list that included temperance, liberality, pride, good temper, truthfulness, and justice. The Boy Scouts emphasized that a scout should be loyal, reverent, clean, honest, and brave. And above all, a scout should "be prepared." Even though this was the scout motto, no scoutmaster ever got around to telling us what we were to be prepared for. Nonetheless, I was impressed by this list of virtues, and at times I did try to do these things. Once in a while I even helped old ladies cross the street. But I was a fairly cooperative boy, rather shy, and not in open rebellion against anyone.

I would be the first to admit that moral knowledge, particularly knowledge of lists of virtues, slogans, Bible verses, and summarized principles of conduct, does not ensure moral conduct. In fact, modern research shows only slight correlations. However, when properly used, and when supplemented with many other methods of teaching, such approaches can help. A full discussion is given in Chapter 5, "Talking and Teaching."

The Hidden Curriculum

Another traditional method of moral teaching is the "hidden curriculum" approach. This method avoids direct moralization and teaches moral values indirectly, primarily through stories. Some of the old stories taught to young children are good examples of this approach. I was always very impressed with the story of the Dog and the Bone. The dog had a bone in his jaws, saw his reflection in a pool of water, thought the dog in the reflection had a bigger bone, and so dropped his to get the larger one. Naturally, he lost the one bone he had. What greed! I was impressed. Many of Aesop's fables and countless other children's stories (the Little Red Hen, the Three Little Pigs, King Midas) had a moral lesson. The once-famous McGuffey readers sought to instill moral virtue through the content of the stories read by young students. Telling stories with a moral lesson is still a favorite method of teaching in church school classes, although children get bored if such lessons contain too much preaching. Success is better assured if students can identify with the characters in the story, and if the story makes a point without undue repetition.

Respect for Authority

The "respect for authority" approach defines moral education in terms of teaching respect for established authority, rules, and current community values. Thus, school pupils are told:

"Do not run in the halls."

"Do not smoke in school."

"Do not waste paper towels."

"Do not chew gum."

"Do not talk when in line."

"Do not cheat on exams."

Like the "bag of virtues" approach, just telling pupils to do (or not do) something does not ensure compliance. But when supplemented by systems of rewards and punishments, the latter approach can and does have an influence on the behavior of most pupils. While morality cannot be equated with the rules of a particular group, the approach can influence children's conduct.

Do Nothing

The "do nothing" approach is used by those parents who are afraid that, if they indoctrinate their children in any religion or system of moral values, the children will rebel against what they have been taught or will develop undesirable religious prejudices. These are the parents who say, "I'm going to wait until my daughter is old enough to decide for herself."

The intention—not to develop individuals with closed minds—is admirable. But the result is different from what parents expect. By "doing nothing" parents are actually "doing something." They are contributing to moral confusion in their children by failing to provide any guidance for moral choices. How can children have any basis for making choices without some prior knowledge and understanding on which wise decisions may be based? I feel it is the task of religious parents to teach their faith and morals to their children and to develop as sharp an understanding as possible; then as youngsters approach their teenage years, they can question, examine, and modify what they have learned according to what seems truth for them. This does not mean that religious instruction should be narrow and bigoted—the kind which doesn't allow different points of view—or that parents should teach their religion as the only right religion. It means simply that parents can bear witness to what has been meaningful to them and what values they hold and why, realizing that each growing young person must at varying times in life sift out what can be believed and lived from what cannot.

PSYCHOLOGICAL AND SOCIOLOGICAL INSIGHTS

Modern psychology and sociology have thrown a great deal of light on how children learn and on the methods and means by which moral growth takes place.

Psychoanalysis

Sigmund Freud taught that people are driven by instinctual urges located in the unconscious *id* (Freud, 1933). The id consists of all the instinctual drives and feelings that persons express unconsciously. Left unchecked, however, such expressions get people into trouble. They do things that hurt others or interfere with their rights, and in so doing they bring criticism, condemnation, and punishment to themselves. Since all normal persons seek pleasure and try to avoid pain, they strive to adjust and act in ways that bring the maximum possible satisfaction with the minimum amount of hurt.

The *ego* is the evaluative, rational power of individuals which enables them to weigh the pros and cons of actions and to make decisions. But since rational power alone is not enough to counteract the forces of the id, another counterforce is needed, the internal restraint of conscience, or the *superego*. The superego represents the sum total of moral do's and don'ts, as interpreted by parents and other important persons. Freud taught that the most critical period for development of the conscience is between five and twelve years of age. During this period, children are most influenced by the actions, words, and attitudes of authority figures.

The task of parents then is to develop their children's superego, or conscience, by emphasizing what they consider to be right and wrong. When children do wrong, parents express disapproval and withdraw love. When children do right, parents praise and accept them. Eventually, children respond to these influences and accept the values they are being taught. They *internalize* these messages and make them their own. When this happens, they are guided by their conscience. They feel guilty and bad when they do wrong, and glad and good when they do right.

As every parent knows, there is much truth to this theory. It can achieve results when applied properly. There are several problems, however in following it closely. First, the values or standards that are taught are usually those most prevalent in society and in the parents' thinking. Freud made no attempt to moralize and say what should or should not be taught. The morality of children will depend largely upon the morality of their parents and influential adults. Children can be taught to feel guilty if they are friendly toward some member of a minority group, for example. Christian parents still face the question: What values should I teach?

Second, some overzealous parents become too rigid and restrictive. They develop the superego to such an extent that their children live with an excessive fear of doing wrong. Their children then go through life as overly inhibited, guilt-ridden persons, never daring to express creativity or individuality for fear of criticism and rejection. They strive so hard to please others that they never please or satisfy themselves. They may have great talent, but it is never expressed. Parents need to be careful, therefore, to achieve a happy medium between extremes of restrictiveness and permissiveness, trying to develop sufficient restraint in their children so they can live as socialized, moral individuals, but allowing them sufficient freedom to make the most of their individual potentials.

Third, while withdrawal of love is effective in controlling children's behavior, it can be quite detrimental to total personality development when carried to extremes. It leaves children feeling rejected, unworthy, unhappy, and without atonement if they feel they never please their parents. Parents need to learn to help their children feel they are loved—even when they do wrong and their behavior is disapproved. Parents need to "hate sin, but love the sinner."

Behaviorism and Operant Conditioning

Harvard University professor B. F. Skinner is one of the chief exponents of a practical method for influencing and modifying human behavior. He calls his method operant conditioning (Skinner, 1971, 1974). An *operant* in Skinner's language is any behavior of a person that modifies the environment in which that person lives. To *condition* an operant means to influence it, to try to effect a change in it, so that this change, in turn, will modify the situation in which a person is placed. For example:

> In one Oregon case, a nine-year-old boy had not been able to move past the second grade level. He spent most of his time misbehaving: talking, pushing, hitting, pinching, squirming and staring around the room. He would sometimes get up and shove his desk around the aisles. Behaviorist Gerald Patterson set up a small light on the boy's desk, and told him that it would flash every ten seconds if he was sitting quietly doing his work. For each flash, the boy earned a penny and an M & M, payable at the end of the lesson. The other kids in class would be paid off with a share of the booty if they did not distract the boy when he was working. After ten days of conditioning, he was misbehaving about 15 percent of the time. That's about average for normal children. (Hilts, 1974)

In this example, the operant is the child's obnoxious behavior, which needs conditioning, needs to be changed or modified. The conditioning is done through use of *reinforcers,* which in this case are the flashing light and the pennies and candies the child receives for proper behavior. The child learns that by doing his work quietly he can bring positive rewards to himself. His antisocial behavior (the operant) is conditioned, or changed, into positive behavior, which in turn changes how others respond to him.

This is really the same principle that parents use when they seek to modify their children's behavior by a control-through-reward approach (Alexander, 1976, p. 195). If used positively and lovingly to accomplish desirable objectives, such an approach can be an effective way of developing desirable habits and behavior. In the laboratory, rats learn to run their mazes to avoid shocks and to receive their pellets of corn. Skinner's pigeons learned to play ping-pong in response to reinforcement procedures. Students can learn to read and write and manipulate numbers on learning machines when right answers are rewarded by appropriate buzzes and flashing lights (Forisha and Forisha, 1976, p. 59). Similarly, children can learn to tell the truth and to be honest, generous, cooperative, grateful, and kind by parental use of positive reinforcement such as praise, privileges, or special recognition in other ways. Of course, children can be conditioned to respond in undesirable, immoral ways also, so the morality of the persons doing the conditioning is important to the total outcome. Much more will be said about this subject in Chapter 6.

Modeling and Social Learning

Social learning is concerned primarily with how environmental factors influence behavior. The primary influence is the example that others set for them. Children observe the behavior of others and seek to imitate them. This process is referred to as *modeling*. As children grow, they imitate different models from their social environment: parents, teachers, peers, entertainment heroes, and others. While being cared for primarily by parents, young children imitate their parents' language, gestures, mannerisms, habits, attitudes, and values. School-age children may repeat a teacher's ideas about social or moral problems in dinner conversations at home. Adolescents are increasingly influenced by entertainment heroes and peers, particularly in such areas as clothing selection, hairstyles, music, speech, food preferences, or basic social values. Imitation is important in learning such behavior as self-control, altruism, aggression, or sexual behavior (Rice, 1978, p. 71).

Two social scientists, Bandura and Walters, showed that when children or adolescents observed aggression in a real-life model, or on film or television, many of the children's responses were accurate imitations of the aggressive acts they had observed in person or on film (Bandura, 1973; Bandura, Ross, and Ross, 1963; Bandura and Walters, 1959). It was shown that boys who tended to be aggressive had parents who were more aggressive toward them, who used more punitive, physical discipline. Bandura writes:

> When a parent punishes his child physically for having aggressed toward peers, for example, the intended outcome of this training is that the child should refrain from hitting others. The child, however, is also learning from parental demonstration how to be aggressive physically. (Bandura and Perloff, 1967, p. 43)

The parents of the most aggressive boys provided a model of aggression. These parents also encouraged their sons to show more aggression outside the home toward other children—to stand up for their rights and to use their fists. Less aggressive sons had parents who limited the amount of aggression they would tolerate. These boys were more controlled by guilt and internal restraints. When the aggressive sons were inhibited at all it was by fear of punishment rather than by guilt and internal controls. Since they did not have as close a relationship with parents, especially with fathers, their conscience development suffered (Bandura and Walters, 1959).

The work of social learning theorists is of great importance in explaining social behavior. What adults do and the role models they represent are far more important in influencing adolescent behavior than what they say. Teachers and parents can best teach human decency, altruism, moral values, and a social conscience by exhibiting these virtues themselves.

EDUCATIONAL PERSPECTIVES

Child Development and Growth

One of the things that child development experts have emphasized is that the growth of children takes place naturally if their needs are met. This is because children have within them what we might call "the seeds of growth," or "the natural tendency to grow." For example, children don't have to be taught to grow physically. They just do. This tendency is so strong that only by extreme physical deprivation can parents prevent physical growth, and even then some development takes place. This means that the parental task is to meet children's physical needs for food, rest, exercise, fresh air, water, and protection from physical harm. If parents supply these needs, children will grow—because that is the way they are made.

The same principle applies to emotional, social, intellectual, and moral growth. Supply what children need and they will grow. They have emotional needs—for love, affection, security, approval, and new experiences. If these needs are supplied, children develop positive feelings of love and security. They have social needs—for companionship and socialization. Children are naturally gregarious. They like to be with others. They want others to like them, but they don't know how to relate or please. So the parental task is to build on the normal desire to belong and to relate by teaching group customs, manners, habits, mores, and values. The tendency to grow intellectually is also inborn. Children are curious by nature. If their curiosity is encouraged, if they are provided with sensory stimulation and a variety of learning experiences through observation, reading, and conversation, they will learn at an unbelievably fast pace.

Children also have the capacity for moral growth. They are born trusting persons. This is partially the meaning of Jesus' saying: "Whoever does not receive the kingdom of God like a child shall not enter it" (Mark 10:15). It is this complete faith that God demands. Children only learn to disbelieve when they discover they can't trust the people around them. Children are also born with the capacity to develop a sensitive conscience, to feel guilt when they do wrong, and to distinguish moral values once taught. Of course, this capacity must be developed through educated reasoning, by imitation, and through experience. The parental role is to fulfill children's needs for trust and values to live by, so that moral growth can take place (Rice, 1979, p. 559).

It is important to realize that parents are working *with* the child's natural tendencies, not against them; working to fulfill children's needs so they can grow. Of course, sometimes children's needs are not met, because parents either cannot or will not fulfill them. Children aren't given proper food or rest; they aren't loved; they aren't socialized; they are deprived intellectually and spiritually. When this happens, growth slows down or stops and children remain physically, emotionally, socially, intellectually, or morally retarded. *Growth takes place when needs are met; retardation occurs through deprivation* (Rice, 1979, p. 559).

Education for Life

John Dewey was one of the first educators to emphasize that what students need is not direct moral instruction, such as admonitions to be honest and truthful, but the opportunity for experiences through which they develop moral habits, affective capacities, and the ability to make moral judgments. Dewey emphasized that the task of education is to provide the conditions for optimal development of the innate or natural capacities of children. In accomplishing this, he conceived of the classroom as a laboratory of living in which children have the chance to participate in carefully selected learning experiences through which they develop cognitive, social, and emotional skills by which they are able to live as moral beings (Cully, 1963, p. 190). Dewey wrote:

> In so far as the school represents in its own spirit, a genuine community life; in so far as what are called school discipline, governments, order, etc., are the expressions of this inherent social spirit; in so far as the methods used are those that appeal to the active and constructive powers, permitting the child to give out and thus to serve; in so far as the

curriculum is so selected and organized as to provide the materials for affording the child a consciousness of the world in which he has to play a part, and the demands he has to meet, so far as these ends are met, the school is organized on an ethical basis. (Dewey, 1909, p. 41)

Dewey felt that the ultimate purpose of all education is the formation of moral character and that this is accomplished primarily through experience. Much more will be said about moral development through doing in Chapter 8.

The Development of Moral Judgment

Moral judgment means the ability to make moral decisions, to distinguish what is right from what is wrong, or what is good from what is not quite so good. The development of this ability is primarily the development of rational and cognitive faculties. We are particularly indebted to two men, Piaget and Kohlberg, for their research and writings which help us to understand the process by which this comes about (Piaget, 1932; Kohlberg, 1969).

One of the educational methods employed is to present real-life situations that involve making moral choices and to encourage students to think about the choices they would make and why they would make them. Here is one example that has been used to stimulate students to employ reason in making moral judgments.

A group of young boys went into a neighborhood candy store every day after school. At first everything was all right, but soon they began to take things without paying for them. One day the owner caught them, and they admitted to him that they had been stealing candy for quite a while. What should he do and why? (Hall and Davis, 1975, p. 132)

In encouraging students to think, the teacher might ask them to think about the various alternatives, such as:

1. Tell their parents
2. Call the police
3. Ask them to work for what they had taken
4. Give a warning—threaten to tell parents if they did it again
5. Spank them and send them home

(Hall and Davis, 1975, pp. 134, 135)

Also the teacher might ask, "What might be likely to happen as a result of each of these courses of action?" By considering the consequences of each course of action, and by evaluating whether or not these effects are desirable or undesirable, the students are encouraged to arrive at a decision that each considers "best" on the basis of logic and reason.

The purpose in presenting this dilemma is not to try to get all students to agree on a decision, but to teach them to think and to use reason in making moral judgments. Here is an example used by Kohlberg in stimulating students to use reason in making moral judgments.

> In Europe, a woman was near death from cancer. One drug might save her, a form of radium that a druggist in the same town had recently discovered. The druggist was charging $2,000, ten times what the drug cost him to make. The sick woman's husband, Heinz, went to everyone he knew to borrow the money, but he could only get together about half what it cost. He told the druggist that his wife was dying and asked him to sell it cheaper or let him pay later. But the druggist said, "No." The husband got desperate and broke into the man's store to steal the drug for his wife. Should the husband have done that? Why? (Kohlberg, 1969)

One of Kohlberg's most important contributions was his description of the stages of moral development through which children, adolescents, and adults pass (Kohlberg, 1969). He outlined three different levels (and six sublevels) at which people make moral decisions (Rice, 1980).

Level I may be identified as a *premoral level,* since little thinking actually takes place. Children who are at this level are well behaved, but in a stereotyped way, since they give unquestioning obedience to their superiors, and since they respond without thinking to what is considered good or bad by their social reference group. Response at this level is egocentric and is motivated by the desire to avoid punishment or the need to gain rewards from others (Peters, 1974, p. 549). Children at this stage judge the morality of an act by the physical consequences regardless of the meaning or value of these consequences.

Level II is best described as a morality of *convention,* in which the goal is conformity, following rules, living up to the expectations, rules, and laws of one's own family, group, or nation in order to avoid guilt feelings and the disapproval and censure of others. This level is less ego-centric than Level I, and more sociocentric, since it is based on a desire to maintain and support the social order.

Level III is morality that emphasizes *universally applicable principles* such as individual rights, human dignity, and equality. These universal principles of justice are considered valid beyond existing laws, social conditions, or peer mores. Therefore, individuals governed by these ethical principles have achieved moral autonomy and feel that they may, under some circumstances, break unjust civil laws because they recognize a morality higher than existing law. In the case of the husband, Heinz, this level of morality might say that he was justified in stealing the drug to save the life of his wife, when all other attempts to obtain it failed, not because it was right to steal, but because the need to save a human life was a moral obligation that took precedence over obedience to laws that protected property. The American soldier who refused orders to participate in the massacre at the Vietnamese village of My Lai in 1968 was identified as being at this level (Fraenkel, 1977, p. 56).

Progression from one of these stages of moral thinking to another cannot be equated with the specific age of a child, although the chances of being at an advanced level of moral thought are greater as one grows older. However, within any one age group, individuals are at different levels of development in their moral thinking. Some are retarded; others are advanced. Part of this is due to the fact that the ability to make moral judgments is partially related to basic intelligence. The great majority of adults in the United States never reach Level III (Rice, 1978, p. 518). Most are at Level II—and live at a conventional, conformist level of morality.

These principles of development of moral judgment have important implications for parents (Rice, 1980).

All young children need rules to follow if they are to behave properly. The younger they are, the more they need the constraint and guidance of parents in doing what is right. Since young children do not have the knowledge of right and wrong or the capacity to make proper judgments, the parents' role is to make these decisions for them by establishing rules and principles to govern their behavior. These rules can be enforced through verbal admonitions and discussions, including reprimands or praise, or by establishing a system of rewards and punishments.

As children get older, they are governed less by hard-and-fast rules and more by a sensitized conscience that reflects parental feelings and desires. They also begin to want to conform to the expectations of their peers in order to avoid the disapproval of others and the censure of their own guilt feelings. Conscience development takes place primarily by interaction with others. It depends upon positive parental attitudes and a family environment that emphasizes warmth and acceptance. It also depends upon extensive peer-group participation in groups that evidence a high level of morality and responsible behavior. Children can learn acceptable principles of moral conduct from such groups. This is why it is wise to expose school-age children to organized groups that exert a positive influence.

Children also learn by having a wide variety of positive experiences as well as the opportunity to discuss alternative forms of behavior and the various options that are open to them in making decisions. Ultimately, parents have to allow older children and youths more and more opportunities to make moral decisions, and to place more responsibilities upon them for the decisions they have made. The goal is to help children accept moral principles for themselves, principles that are arrived at in reciprocal relationships with other people, where out of mutual respect they begin to treat others as they themselves would wish to be treated. Thus they pass from a *morality of constraint,* one that depends upon external restraints, to a *morality of cooperation,* where they do the right thing out of concern for the feelings and welfare of others (Piaget, 1932).

4
Learning Through Intimacy

EMOTIONS AND BEHAVIOR

One of the tasks of parents and teachers is to help children and young people develop the right kind of emotions. The word "emotion" literally means "the act of being moved out, or stirred up." Emotions are what people feel in response to different stimuli.

Emotions are important because they affect behavior in relationships with others. How people feel partially controls how they act. Those who feel loving act more kindly toward others. Those who feel angry may seek to strike out at others. Those who are afraid often become defensive and unreasonable. People express their feelings in their everyday relationships with other people. What and how they feel is an important influence on their behavior.

Recently, newspapers carried headlines of a father and his twelve-year-old son, both of whom had been shot by a sixteen-year-old boy. Their bodies were found in the woods covered over with leaves. The father had been shot thirty-two times. What prompted such rage and violence? The exact causes were never discovered, but obviously the boy was deeply disturbed emotionally. His emotional disturbance, which he must have carried around with him since childhood, resulted in his committing these acts of extreme violence.

One of the major tasks of moral education is to help children and adolescents develop the right kinds of feelings. If young people *feel* right about themselves, other people, and the world—inside—they are more likely to *do* right.

THE DEVELOPMENT OF FEELINGS

Feelings have their origin in the intimate relationships that children experience while growing up. The development of warm, affectionate, caring, optimistic, and happy feelings comes from a secure environment, pleasurable events, and close interpersonal relationships in which children's needs are met.

Levels of Need

These needs have been ranked in five levels, ascending from physiological to psychological. These levels are:

Level 1. *Physiological*—Need for food, water, air, and warmth

Level 2. *Safety*—Need to escape from dangers and threats

Level 3. *Love and Affection*—Need to receive love, care, and attention

Level 4. *Interpersonal Relationships*—Need to belong, to be valued, accepted, respected by others, and to feel self-esteem and worth

Level 5. *Achievement and Self-Expression*—Need to be creative and productive, and to realize one's potentials

(Maslow, 1968)

Children must first satisfy those needs which are lower in the hierarchy, since these are essential to physical life.

As these needs are supplied, children experience positive feelings of comfort, satisfaction, and well-being. If they should be denied basic physical requirements and protection from physical harm, they experience hunger, thirst, cold, pain, and other physical discomforts. Along with these physical discomforts they feel frustration, fear, anxiety, anger, or hostility (Rice, 1978, p. 195). As long as they feel this way, it is almost impossible for them to be kind, trusting, and loving toward others. This is why children must first satisfy those needs which arc lower in the hierarchy before they are ready to move on to satisfy higher needs.

At higher levels they seek to satisfy their needs for love and affection, companionship, approval, acceptance, and respect. If these emotional needs are supplied, their capacity to show positive feelings toward others grows and they become loving, affectionate, friendly, companionable, caring, accepting, respecting persons. If these needs are not supplied, then their capacity to show healthy emotions in relationship with others is severely limited.

Emotional Deprivation

The effects of emotional deprivation upon children have been well documented. One author describes the reactions of a two-year-old who had to be hospitalized and who was subsequently neglected by his mother. He was looked after by a nurse and visited by his mother during the first week, but his behavior deteriorated when the mother reduced her visits to twice a week and then gave up visiting him.

> He became listless, often sat in a corner sucking and dreaming, at other times he was very aggressive. He almost completely stopped talking. . . . He sat in front of his plate eating very little, without pleasure, and started smearing his food

over the table. At this time, the nurse who had been looking after him fell ill, and Bobby did not make friends with anyone else, but let himself be handled by everyone without opposition. A few days later he had tonsillitis and went to the sickroom. In the quiet atmosphere there he seemed not quite so unhappy, played quietly but generally gave the impression of a baby. He hardly ever said a word, had entirely lost his bladder and bowel control, sucked a great deal. On his return to the nursery he looked very pale and tired. He was very unhappy after rejoining the group, always in trouble and in need of help and comfort. He did not seem to recognize the nurse who had looked after him at first. (Bowlby, 1965, p. 30)

The important consideration is that if emotional deprivation continues for long, the effects carry over into adolescence and have a marked influence on adolescent behavior. Youths who are rejected as children may become cold, insensitive, uncaring individuals who lack sensitivity to others and whose consciences never fully develop. In extreme instances, they become completely unfeeling persons who don't even experience guilt when they hurt others or do wrong.

The Development of Love and Affection

One of the most interesting demonstrations of how love, affection, and sensitivity develop or do not develop was given by the psychologist Harlow in his research with monkeys (Harlow, 1958; Harlow and Suomi, 1970). The monkeys that he studied were reared from infancy to adulthood under various conditions: some by their own mothers and others by mechanical substitute mothers. In one experiment, four baby monkeys received their milk from the artificial breast of a wire mother; four other baby monkeys received their milk from the artificial breast of a cloth mother. Both groups had access to both mothers at times other than when fed, and both preferred the cloth mother. They would run to her when frightened, cling to her, and seek comfort through contact with her. Harlow felt that the "contact comfort" a baby derived from its mother was important in developing affectional responses (Harlow, 1958, p. 676).

All eight monkeys fed by artificial mothers did not do nearly as well as those raised by their natural mothers. The artificially reared monkeys seemed to thrive as babies, but by the time they reached adulthood they failed or had difficulty developing normal social relationships and showing normal affectionate responses and sex behavior. They fought viciously; the males and females did not mate as monkeys normally do. The few females who did become mothers were "helpless, hopeless, heartless mothers devoid or almost devoid of any maternal feeling" (Harlow, 1962).

The important point is that by the time children reach adolescence they already exhibit well-developed patterns of emotional response to events and people. They may already be described as warm, affectionate, and friendly, or as cold, unresponsive, and distant. The pattern of emotional response shown during adolescence is only a continuation of the pattern that has been emerging slowly from childhood (Rice, 1978, p. 196).

Adolescents who become affectionate, friendly people have some distinct advantages. Not only do they derive far greater personal satisfaction from human relationships, but their social relationships are more harmonious. Love encourages a positive response from others; it minimizes aggressive behavior in oneself and others; it acts as a therapeutic force in healing hurts; it is a creative power in individual accomplishment and in social movements. It stimulates human vitality and longevity; it is the driving force in positive biological and social relationships in marriage. It is necessary as a binding power in friendships or in adolescents' relationships with their parents.

SELF-CONCEPT

Another important influence on the behavior of adolescents comes from the attitudes and feelings which they have about themselves. When they perceive themselves, what value do they place on the selves they perceive? Does this appraisal lead to self-acceptance and approval, to a feeling of self-worth?

Adolescents with low self-esteem are vulnerable to criticism, rejection, and to any evidence that testifies to their inadequacy, incompetence, or worthlessness. They are disturbed when laughed at, reprimanded, or depreciated in any way. Such adolescents report: "I can't stand criticism, or to have anyone make fun of me."

One reaction is to try to develop a false front or facade with which to impress the world. As one young person expressed it: "I try to put on an act to impress people." Some adolescents try to become the toughest or meanest. Others gain recognition by bragging or showing off. Others strive to be the most daring, or the wildest. Some want to be the sexiest, others the handsomest, still others the smartest. Adolescents with inadequate self-concepts are more likely to be involved in delinquent acts as a way to compensate for personal feelings of inadequacy. In fact, research has shown a close relationship between delinquency and lack of self-esteem (Schwartz and Tangri, 1965). It is difficult to be a moral person when one is continually trying to compensate for feelings of inadequacy or worthlessness.

Those with poor self-concepts have great difficulty in

their social adjustments. They may overreact to what others say about them. They are on the defensive to protect their fragile egos. They tend to be jealous, unstable persons who are difficult to get along with. They are selfish and inconsiderate of the rights of others since they are always wrapped up in themselves and their problems.

Some youths with inferiority complexes withdraw from the social scene and are outstanding only in their social invisibility. They are not noticed or selected as leaders, and do not as often participate in class, club, or social activities. They often feel self-conscious and awkward in social situations, don't know what to say or how to act. Because they are so anxious to please or be noticed, they are more easily influenced and led, and thus they more often get into trouble. They are less apt to like other people and to trust them. Since they lack self-respect or self-confidence, they are more likely to hate, envy, despise, and distrust others. These feelings are a real handicap in trying to relate to others in mature, positive, and moral ways (Rice, 1978, p. 221).

The Adult Task

The adult task is to help adolescents build adequate self-concepts and self-esteem. But how? The primary way is by showing love, approval, admiration, and acceptance of them, since their feelings about themselves are largely a mirror of how they interpret what others, and especially parents, feel about them. Elder writes:

> If children are going to be well-adjusted, psychologically and emotionally, they must be held in special regard by their parents, family, teachers, and other adults who interact with them in any way. When due respect is given to them and taught to them, they in turn will respond with respect to others. (Elder, 1976, p. 29)

Parents who frequently express disapproval and criticism make children unsure of themselves. Such parents are showing their children that they actually dislike them. Two psychiatrists describe the life of a boy whose parents hate him:

> From the time he awakens in the morning until he goes to bed at night he is nagged, scolded, and frequently slapped. His attempts at conversation are received with curt, cold silence or he is told to be quiet. If he attempts to show any demonstration of affection, he is pushed away and told not to bother his parents. He receives no praise for anything he does no matter how well he had done it. If he walks with his parents and lags a little, his arm is seized and he is yanked forward. If he falls, he is yanked to his feet. . . . At mealtimes he is either ignored or his table manners and inconsequential food fads are criticized severely. He is made to finish whatever is on his plate. . . .
>
> The child soon realizes that he can expect nothing but a hurt body or hurt feelings from his parents, and instead of feeling love for them, he feels fear, loathing, and hatred. (English and Pearson, 1945, p. 108)

If criticism continues over the years, the results can be disastrous. Such criticism destroys whatever self-confidence teenagers have in themselves. It may stimulate such resentment and anger that the adolescent is driven to acts of vandalism and violence.

HOSTILITY AND ANGER

Whenever excessive anger builds up that cannot be expressed in constructive ways or be contained, it may take impulsive, irrational, and destructive forms and the adolescent becomes a menace. This is one explanation of the wanton violence and vandalism in which some young people become involved. Anger that turns into destructive ple become involved. Anger that turns into destructive violence usually builds up through repeated incidents. A father may reject, belittle, or treat his son cruelly for years before the son's anger explodes in an act of violence (Rice, 1978, p. 205).

Hostility or hatred can be an even more serious emotion than anger (at least temporary anger) because it persists over a longer period of time because of repeated exposure to particular persons. The following is an example of such hatred, and is expressed by a college male toward his father.

Elizabeth Barrett Browning once wrote a sonnet in which she expressed the love she had for her husband Robert. The poem begins with the words: "How do I love thee? Let me count the ways." Inspired by these immortal words, I have thought about writing a similar poem about my father. A more appropriate opening to the poem would be, "How do I HATE thee? Let me count the ways." I would continue from there to write one of the longest poems in the history of literature. Each verse would start with a different reason for hating him. In verse one, I could expound on how frequently he comes home drunk and raises hell. Verse two could elaborate on his disgusting behavior while sober. Verse three could revolve around the fact that he keeps a disproportionate amount of his salary for himself at the expense of his family. After I wrote about two hundred verses, material for the poem would finally begin to run out.

My present ambition is to kick my father's head in. Unfortunately, this ambition cannot be realized because I depend on him for support while I am going to college. I have sublimated my hostile feelings toward him by developing a fantasy in which I knock his block off. Accordingly, I propose that the first order of business on graduation day is to gently take off my father's glasses and then proceed to punch hell out of him. (Donovan, 1975, pp. 85, 86)

Obviously, such hatred is extreme, but as long as it exists it will prevent that son from ever relating in a positive way to his father.

POSITIVE CONSIDERATIONS

What can or should parents and other adults do? The best solution is prevention: to relate in such positive ways to children and youths that only positive and healthy emotions develop. This does not mean that adolescents will never get mad or upset. But it means that the predominant climate of adult-teenage relationships is warm, accepting, and loving—not rejecting, critical, or hateful. Really the only way to develop loving persons is in an atmosphere of warmth, affection, and love.

I remember an old movie in which a stern but pious father was administering discipline to his son with a stiff willow switch. Each time he hit the boy he repeated: "Love God, love God." This is certainly *not* the way to teach children to love God or one another.

If the adolescent is already filled with excessive anger or hostility because of real or imagined wrongs, adults will need to take remedial action. If the problem is severe, counseling help for both the teenager and the parents is in order. If the problem is one that parents feel they can handle, the most appropriate way is through discussion— sitting down and talking it out. But parents will find adolescents much more willing to cooperate if the adults first listen to what their adolescents want to tell them. One of the best ways to relieve feelings is to talk them out, provided the discussion takes place within the limits of respect and consideration for the other party. Of course, unrestrained name-calling and criticism add fuel to the fires of resentment, so parents need to insist on honest discussion, but within civilized, courteous boundaries. If adolescents can't or won't talk to parents, the discussion may take place with a clergyman, teacher, or counselor.

To deny or to repress intense feeling is almost impossible and certainly unhealthy. But to express any and all feelings without any control and without regard for the rights and feelings of others is also undesirable. Adolescents living together with others can't expect unlimited expression of emotion. If they try it, they hurt themselves as well as others.

The answer is neither suppression nor complete indulgence, but controlled expression in socially acceptable ways. Some of these are suggested below.

Physical activity. Whether through work or recreation, physical activity is a fine way of releasing pent-up feelings.

Verbalizing. Talking out one's feelings is acceptable unless the language becomes abusive. It also helps one to feel better.

Laughing. Humor relieves many tense situations. Being able to laugh at oneself, with others, and at tense times is helpful emotional catharsis.

Crying. In some situations crying is permissible and accepted. Honestly expressed tears provide enormous relief for pent-up feelings.

Affection. The expression of affection is especially helpful in relieving tension. Hugging, kissing, and other forms of expression relieve anxiety and other natural emotions by replacing them with positive feelings of security, satisfaction, and love (Rice, 1978, p. 210).

Emotions properly expressed ought to make the individual a calmer, happier, better-adjusted person. Learning both how to express and how to control feelings is a necessary part of becoming a morally mature person.

5

Talking and Teaching

FACTUAL BIBLICAL INSTRUCTION

Uniform Lessons

In the early 1860's, a Methodist minister by the name of John Vincent decided that the lack of uniform curriculum materials for Sunday school made the teaching of lessons and values a haphazard venture (Lannie, 1975, p. 120). Consequently, he developed standardized lesson plans for all children and also established teacher training institutes.

Vincent's first published plans were entitled *Little Footprints in Bible Lands; or, Simple Lessons in Sacred History and Geography, for the Use of Palestine Classes and Sabbath Schools,* and came complete with maps and gazetteer, questions and answers, charts and hymns, graded readings, and suggested rewards. Here is Lesson I:

Lesson I. BIBLE LANDS

Teacher: What is Sacred Geography?
Children: A description of sacred places on the earth.
Teacher: Of what parts of the earth does sacred geography treat?
Children: Of those countries mentioned in the Bible; also called Bible lands.

Teacher: Where do they lie?
Children: In Europe, Asia, and Africa, principally in Asia.
Teacher: Name the most important of these countries.
Children: (The children chant, using tune on p. 107): Ar-
menia, Media, Parthia, Persia, Chaldea (also
called Shinar and Babylonia), Arabia, Philistia,
Mesopotamia, Assyria, Phoenicia, Syria, Canaan,
Egypt, Libya, Ethiopia, Spain, Italy, Greece, and
Asia Minor.

(Vincent, 1861, p. 8)

By merrily chanting, the children learned the most important countries in Bible lands. They gradually trod through
Palestine and were rewarded for their progression by
moving from the "Pilgrim" stage to those of "Resident,"
"Explorer," "Dweller in Jerusalem," and at last "Tem-
plar." "Sacred biography was full of character and incident," reasoned Vincent, "and sacred geography alive
with interest."

Vincent began publishing *The Sunday School Teacher*
and included in the monthly issues a new scheme of uniform lessons entitled *Two Years with Jesus: A New System
of Sunday-School Study.* It was a two-year system composed of twenty-four lessons per year. Lessons extended
over a two-week period, the remaining four weeks were
for review, and prayer. In the first year children learned
about the life, journeys, and miracles of Jesus; in the second year they studied the parables, conversations, and
discourses of Jesus. There were the "Four P's" and the
"Four D's" by which every teacher and child could prepare the lesson (Lannie, 1975, p. 121). The following questions were used with all the lessons:

1. P. P.   PARALLEL PASSAGES. Is the incident, parable,
conversation, or discourse of the lesson, or anything like
it, elsewhere given in Scripture?
2. P.   PERSONS (Biographical). Who wrote this lesson,

and to whom? What persons are mentioned, and what do you know about them?

3. P.   PLACES (Topographical). Where did these persons live? Places mentioned in the lessons? Where situated? Size, distance, and direction from Jerusalem?

4. D.   DATES (Chronological). In what year of the world and of Christ did these things occur? Age of persons mentioned? Allusion to days, hours, seasons, etc.

5. D.   DOINGS (Historical). What did each person of the lesson do? Who had the most to do? Why?

6. D.   DOCTRINES (Theological). What truths about God, man, character, conduct, the future, and the present are here taught?

7. D.   DUTIES (Practical). What duties to God, man, self, to church, nation, neighbor, enemy, friends, world, old, young, good, and bad, are here taught?

(Vincent, 1887, p. 348)

These lessons were uniform (based on the same Bible passage) for all ages, but were also "graded" because Vincent insisted that the lessons be adapted to the capacities of the pupils.

Vincent emphasized the need for professional Sunday school teachers and established teacher training institutes throughout the country. He also organized a Sunday School Normal College with a course of study that included five textbooks, a program of objectives for ten weekly meetings and a commencement exercise complete with the "Normal Class Vow":

> I do solemnly promise to devote myself with all diligence to Sunday School labor. I will endeavor to study the Word of God more thoroughly and prayerfully, to spend more time in reading, meditation and prayer with special reference to my work . . . , to visit my scholars as their temporal and spiritual necessities may require and to be punctually present at school and all meetings of teachers. (Vincent, 1872, p. 140)

After reciting the vow, graduates received a diploma testifying that they had met the standards of a qualified Sunday school teacher. They were now professional Christian educators who entered into the army of the Lord with Jesus as their leader. Each was now an officer in "the Saviour's Army" and prepared to lead his or her own "Sunday School Brigade." They were ready to march to Zion and stand at the river "that flows by the throne of God" (Lannie, 1975, p. 125).

Vincent is most famous for his Chautauqua movement, which was founded in the 1870's, partly as a teacher training institute for religious educators, and eventuated into a highly successful adult education institution (Vincent, 1886). At one teacher institute on Lake Chautauqua, Vincent outdid himself as he undertook a vivid portrayal of the Holy Land. Here is a description:

> On the shores of the lake, which to him represented the Mediterranean, he caused to be built a topographical map of Palestine, laid out to precise scale, complete with a water-filled and tadpole-infested declivity called the Dead Sea. For good measure, a man named A. O. Van Lennep was engaged to walk among the hills of Palestine as "an Eastern shepherd" in full Oriental costume. (Ferguson, 1971, p. 319)

Vincent was a devout and enthusiastic man who engaged in such projects for the single purpose of preparing outstanding Sunday school teachers.

Critique

As I look back upon my early childhood experiences in Sunday school, I realize the extent to which Vincent's "Bible facts" approach permeated the whole Sunday school movement. We made topographical maps of Palestine out of a paste of salt and flour. We drew charts of Paul's journeys, and we memorized the books of the Bible until we could recite them almost with one breath. Fortunately, along with the facts we learned Bible stories, beginning with Adam and Eve, Cain and Abel, Noah, Abraham, Isaac, Jacob, Joseph, Moses, Joshua, Samson, David, Solomon, and the prophets; and continuing on through the stories of the New Testament. We used creative activities a great deal; also maps, coloring books, time charts, cut-outs, scrapbooks, stand-up figures, flannelgraphs, and certainly drama and music. Everything possible was done to teach us the Bible—its history, geography, stories, and characters.

I have to admit though that the primary emphasis was on Biblical facts—rather than on the messages of the stories and their application to our own lives. I could tell you the story of Jonah and the Whale or Daniel in the Lions' Den by heart, but I could not tell you the central meaning of those stories, why they were included in the Sacred Scriptures, and the religious lessons to be learned from them. It is a great temptation for parents and teachers to become involved in Biblical facts and stories, but to omit matters of doctrine and faith and the central core and message of each of the stories that are told. Why are the stories included? What lessons need to be learned? How does this apply to our lives today? The Bible is filled with stories of real people and events. It also contains many allegories and "for instances" which are included to teach great truths (the story of Jonah is such a story). To teach the story without teaching its central message is to miss the whole reason why the story should be told. It is easy to learn the story, but not as easy to apply it to living. Yet without such application faith, values, and commitment may be affected little, if at all.

I remember a research team that gave standardized tests of Biblical knowledge to a group of college students and then to the inmates of a state penitentiary. The inmates scored higher on the test than the college students! The reason was that the prison chaplain had been spending a great deal of time teaching Bible stories to the prisoners. Since it was a way to get out of their cells, many attended the class. But their acquisition of Biblical knowledge had not altered their basic character and behavior.

Catechisms and Creeds

Prior to the Protestant Reformation, numerous attempts had been made to offer various types of manuals and confessional booklets, primarily for use of priests. These books offered teaching in the elements of the faith, with brief explanations of the Creed, the Lord's Prayer, the Ten Commandments, and the sacraments. There were no manuals for the instruction of children, since this was left to the discretion of parents (Cully, 1963, p. 86).

It was Martin Luther who first attempted to give clear, concise, and brief summaries of Christian doctrine for common people and for children. He published a Large Catechism for the use of pastors and teachers and a Small Catechism for children. Luther's work was of great significance, since it awakened the churches to the need for the systematic training of the young in Christian doctrine.

Three other catechisms arose out of the Reformation: Calvin's Genevan Catechism, the Heidelberg Catechism, and the Prayer Book Catechism of the Church of England. In many Presbyterian churches, these catechisms yielded place to the Larger and Shorter Catechisms of the Westminster Assembly after 1647. The Roman Church at the Council of Trent decided to issue its own catechism, *Catechismus Romanus,* which led to a subsequent production of many others designed more for use by the common people and by children.

The advantages of catechetical instruction are several. It attempts to pinpoint and summarize the most important doctrines and teachings. Catechetical instruction and the use of creeds have always been the primary means of teaching children doctrine, since they are verbal digests of the central truths of the Christian faith. These truths are expressed quite concisely in question and answer form, with attempts made in the children's catechisms to express profound truths in as simple a way as possible so that young minds can understand.

The chief disadvantage to the catechisms is in the way they are used. Here again, the primary emphasis has been on memorization, on learning the right answers word for word, without enough attempt being made to explain the meaning and significance of the words that are learned.

When I was a student at Princeton Theological Seminary, any student who memorized the Shorter Catechism was awarded a hundred-dollar prize. A thoughtful alumnus made these awards possible through an endowment fund. There were no provisions, however, for explaining the meaning of what was memorized or taking an exam to test our understanding of the catechism. Thus, one could repeat the entire catechism by rote without really understanding it, and certainly without one's commitment to Christ, behavior, or values being affected by it. This particular catechism devotes a lot of space to a discussion of the Ten Commandments, and in a very helpful way. Only one professor, so far as I can remember, discussed the catechetical explanations of the meaning and application of the commandments to our lives. However, I found these catechetical explanations helpful and later used them in church school teaching of adolescents. This experience convinced me that proper use of the catechism can be a very helpful way for students to understand the meaning of the Decalogue, which is itself certainly one of the most important summaries of ethical teachings in the Bible.

The same principle applies to the use of creeds: Memorize them, yes, but explain them, discuss them, help adolescents understand their purpose and meaning. Only in this way can their repetition as part of worship really be significant. When students repeat, "I believe in God the Father Almighty . . . ," what does this really mean? What are they really saying? Of what significance is this in living the Christian life? The recital of Christian doctrines demands an intellectual and emotional response: "I believe," "I understand," "I am committed"; therefore "I do."

PROBLEMS WITH WORDS

Children and adolescents do *not* understand the meaning of many words—particularly religious words—that adults take for granted. At one point in my career I was minister of Christian education of a large parish in Brooklyn, New York. We had a fine program of religious instruction, including a released-time weekday religious education program called "Adventure Hour." One afternoon while reciting the Lord's Prayer a third-grader, instead of saying "lead us not into temptation," was pleading "lead us not into Penn Station." Penn Station was real to that child; she had been there. Temptation was no doubt equally real, and she had experienced that too, but the word was not real. The word was a difficult and abstract symbol for a real experience. On another occasion, a child was repeating, "Our Father who art in heaven, hollered be thy name." What on earth does "hallowed" mean to a child anyhow?

In the early 1950's, a mother reported that her child had come home from Sunday school and was quite excited about the new Bible (the Revised Standard Version) which her teacher had shown her. "Oh, Mother," the child exclaimed. "It's beautiful. It's the new Reverse Vision!"

How often do words—words that are symbols of great and profound truths—stand in the way of understanding divine mysteries? God is omnipotent, omnipresent, and omniscient. But what do these concepts mean to adolescents? God is also Lord, light, holy, love. What is the significance of these concepts for our lives? Some of the most important truths are wrapped up in the most abstract and symbolic words. God is a Spirit. What does this mean?

Sometimes we try to express these great truths in physical symbols: a dove, for example, represents the Holy Spirit. Three intertwined rings or a three-leaf shamrock may be used to represent the Trinity, the three equal persons in the Godhead. A hand becomes the creative power of God the Father. Studies have shown that young children do not have the capacity to understand the religious meaning of these physical symbols. Children are not able to understand the messages of political cartoons until about junior high age; the symbolism and message just escapes them before this age. The reason is that children are literalists; they accept literally what is said or drawn, without having the intellectual capacity to understand that there is a deeper meaning.

I remember one minister who in a children's sermon was patiently explaining how each child is an important part of the church. To illustrate this fact the minister had brought a brick and explained that it took hundreds of bricks to make up the walls of the church, and that each and every brick had a part and was important. "In the same way," the pastor explained, "each person, each child, is an important part of the church. All are needed to make up the whole church." But when the child went home, his grandmother asked, "What did you learn in the children's sermon this morning?" The child replied, "I'm a brick." He remembered the physical symbol, but did not understand the religious message. It is important, therefore, to use physical symbols only with those ages which are capable of understanding. Word symbols must be used just as cautiously, since their meaning is often obscure or ambiguous, so that students don't really understand what is being said.

Saying and Doing

There is another problem with words. Every parent knows that just because you say something doesn't mean that young people will do it. You can tell them something, but that doesn't mean you have "taught" it or that students have "learned" it. Saying and doing are two different things—even assuming that understanding has also occurred.

One study of the relationship between moral beliefs and delinquent behavior brought this out clearly (Gannon, 1967). This study was conducted with a sample of boys who had been processed through a juvenile detention home in Cook County, Illinois. Only a small fraction of this group believed that stealing was all right. But of the majority who generally disapproved of stealing, almost one third had several times stolen items worth up to fifty dollars, and another third had several times stolen items worth over fifty dollars. Over half said they would not hesitate to "borrow" a car, and had done so with some regularity. Similarly, while almost three fourths said they would always or usually refuse if their gang wanted them to go along with something they knew was wrong, still almost half of the group had gone along when the group went stealing,

fighting, or causing general disorder. Over half the total
group attended church, some more often than their parents. Most of the group felt they ought to go to church
every Sunday. In addition, the study showed little difference between delinquents and nondelinquents in their
attitude toward God. On tests of religious and moral orthodoxy, the delinquent group revealed a basic theoretical
knowledge of the doctrines of their faith, except for a lack
of awareness of God as a person who is interested in them
individually (Gannon, 1967, p. 429).

What caused the marked inconsistency between the
boys' religious values and their related behaviors? One
reason may be that the boys' religious commitment was
marginal. All had been baptized as infants; their initial
commitments were made for them by their parents. Their
religion was not their own; it was something received as
desirable, but impersonal. There may have been no personal relationship between the individual and his God.
The parental influence was ambiguous (since so many parents did not attend church); thus, the adolescents were
surrounded by ineffectual adult models. At the same time,
the youths were often under the direct influence of their
own peer groups—and the influence was many times negative. Therefore, religion was not a crucial factor in influencing behavior, because it was impersonal and not
supported by other influences immediately crucial to the
delinquent. Gannon concludes:

> The effectiveness of religion depends upon the internaliza-
> tion of standards during the critical formative years of child-
> hood, and is developed through close identification with
> parents, family members, and other significant primary
> groups. Much of this control is exercised unconsciously and
> depends largely upon behavioral examples and religious
> experience rather than on precept. Only later does it reach

the level of conscious decision and personal commitment.

If other supporting controlling agencies are missing, this simply means that the church has encountered a difficulty in coping with factors in modern life that tend to neutralize the fundamental tenets of religious teaching. (Gannon, 1967, p. 429)

These findings make it clear that religious and moral education require more than just telling youths what to believe or how to live, what is right or what is wrong. A lesson is not really learned until it is heard, understood, accepted, and lived by the hearer. I will never forget spending a full hour with junior high youths talking to them about proper behavior in the church. The church was God's house, a sacred place of worship, and we should show awe and respect, and treat the church building and property with reverence. By the end of the hour I was convinced I had taught the class very well. Upon dismissal, the group stampeded out of the room and almost ran me down at the door! They had the "right" answers, but they had not learned the lesson. What can parents and teachers do? There are several things.

1. As already emphasized, make sure the meaning is clear.

2. Don't just tell, discuss. Use feedback from youths to determine what they have learned and how they react to what they have heard. What do they honestly think? Of course, if they are to tell adults, those adults have to learn to listen, to be shockproof, and to be tolerant of various points of view. This doesn't mean adults have to agree, but they should be willing to listen. If they aren't, they'll never discover what their young people think.

3. Ask searching questions that stimulate youth to think more deeply. One mistake parents and teachers make is to ask questions of the "teeth-pulling" sort: questions with

which they are trying to extract a set answer (Hall and Davis, 1975, p. 152). One adolescent complained: "My parents urge me to tell them what I think. Then when I tell them, they say, 'You couldn't really believe that,' and then they keep urging me to answer the way they think I should." Some parents are never satisfied until their young people agree with them completely and tell them they are right. One author emphasizes that the major function of religious education is not to answer questions for adolescents, but to ask them, thus confronting youths with the task of finding their religious identities. He writes: "This is what religious education is all about—understanding the basic questions and seeing that they are asked" (Engel, 1968).

4. Give youths an opportunity to discuss real-life problems which they are facing. Here are some examples:

Under what circumstances should a girl get an abortion? Is abortion ever right?

If a boy gets a girl pregnant, should he marry her?

If a friend asks you for answers on an exam, should you help him to cheat?

Should parents ever get divorced?

Should you associate with others who frequently shoplift?

If a young man opposes war, is he justified in not registering for the draft, or in burning his draft card?

Is it right for a person to cheat on his income tax if he donates all the money he saves to the church?

Would a high school student be justified in selling pot to raise money for college tuition?

By giving youths a chance to discuss such real-life problems, we stimulate them to evaluate their own moral values and to learn how to think about making moral decisions. How they answer also gives adults a clue to what youths are thinking and what ideas need to be brought up to help them grow in their understanding of moral principles.

5. Give youths a chance to put into practice what they have learned. (See Chapter 8, "Learning Through Doing.") I will never forget some of the things that our mother did to try to impress upon us the importance of being honest. On one occasion my brother and I found a large number of redeemable coupons in the trash bin behind a local grocery store. Of course, these coupons had already been redeemed by the grocer and thrown away. But we gathered them up and were able to obtain several dollars' worth of free merchandise—which in this case was candy. Mother was suspicious about the amount of candy we brought home and managed to get us to tell her what we had done. The first thing we had to do was to go back to the storekeeper and confess our thievery to him and apologize. This was by far the hardest and most humiliating thing I had ever had to do. But then we also had to work to earn enough money (at 35 cents an hour) to pay the storekeeper for all the candy we had obtained. As I recall, this in itself amounted to several weeks' work. It was a lesson on honesty I shall never forget.

Parents have to do more than just tell children and youths what is right or wrong. Parents have to expect them to do the right thing, and to put those teachings into practice in their everyday lives. Ways and means of reinforcing the right will be discussed in the next chapter.

6
Positive Reinforcement and Discipline

THE ESTABLISHMENT OF CONTROL

The Need for Control

One distraught mother complained:

> I've tried my best to teach my children right from wrong.
> Since they were little I've spent hours teaching them such
> things as respect for other people's property, the need to
> respect parents and other adults, why they shouldn't use
> swear words, and the importance of basic honesty and tell-
> ing the truth. I've tried to bring them up to consider the
> rights and feelings of others, and to be moral people. But
> just yesterday the grocer at the corner store called and said
> our 13-year-old girl had been caught shoplifting. She took a
> candy bar and a teen magazine off the counter. I'm so
> ashamed. I really don't know what I should do.

This mother is discovering what all parents learn eventually: that the time comes when the moral education of
children must go beyond talking and include enforcement
and discipline. In other words, it must include some form
of control. Cully writes:

> The word discipline still carries implicitly and properly in
> it the idea of control. Through discipline a child develops
> the kind of control that . . . enables him to become more

aware of others, more spiritually attuned. (Cully, 1963, p. 202)

External Control

The younger the child and the more undisciplined, the more external control will have to be used. The research by Kohlberg and Piaget discussed in Chapter 3 makes it clear that moral growth begins with externally imposed control. A child hits another unfairly; the parents reprimand the child and stop the hitting. A child takes something that belongs to another; the parents say "no," they take it away and give it back. Through such means children learn what is allowed and not allowed, what is expected and what is forbidden. In the beginning, their behavior is controlled by others wiser than they, but through this control children begin to learn right from wrong. This type of training is necessary because it lays a foundation of habit and response upon which a child's later self-discipline can be built (Taylor, 1975, p. 149).

As children get older, parents rely less and less on physical restraints such as putting a child in a playpen and more on verbal restraints, and on control by the establishment of a system of rewards and punishments.

Rewards

Let us suppose that a boy finds a wallet with money in it. He decides to return it, and, in exchange, the owner compliments him: "You are a wonderful boy to be so honest." The boy feels pride in himself and experiences a warm feeling inside (Harris, 1976, p. 124). If the owner gives him a reward, he feels doubly blessed. Then when he gets home and his parents learn what he has done, he becomes the object of their special attention and love. "We're pleased at what you've done. Here's a big hug and kiss. Mother is going to cook your favorite supper to show you how proud we are of you." All these things together —praise, recognition, the monetary reward, the special attention and love the parents give, plus the favorite dinner—make the boy glad he returned the wallet, and act as a positive reinforcement, as a stimulus for performing subsequent acts of honesty. Most children need some incentives for doing what is considered "right" or "good." Eventually as "right" becomes habitual, the self-satisfaction gained becomes the reward and motivation (Rice, 1980). If "right" habits have been well enough established, the child is self-disciplined and external controls are no longer necessary.

Punishments

Before this time comes, however, adults will also have to establish some punishments for violations of rules and moral standards. Suppose a girl tells a lie. Her parents find out about it, give her a scolding and reprimand, and send her to her room for an hour. She feels anxious and guilty because she has done wrong and her parents are angry with her; she misses their presence and approval and she regrets her actions because she cannot leave her room. All these factors make her regret her action and build her resolve not to lie to her parents again (Rice, 1980).

Guilt such as the girl experienced in the above example is necessary in order to prevent subsequent wrongdoing (Forisha and Forisha, 1976, p. 23). The guilt was stimulated by a combination of punishments, including the verbal reprimand, the loss of approval of parents, and the restriction of activity and freedom. Since all normal children seek love and approval, they will ordinarily try to adjust their behavior to win such approval. If they do wrong, they lose approval. They will be unhappy, and stimulated to modify their actions the next time.

Scolding or disapproval has a real advantage over physical punishment such as spanking. Disapproval is not a quick and tangible punishment. The feelings of regret remain, leaving a child with unhappy memories that can only be removed by trying to get back into the good graces of parents by trying to please them. Isolation in his or her room also gives the child a chance to think about the wrongdoing, and it stimulates a resolve to do better in the future.

Of course, disapproval can be counterproductive and destructive to the child's ego if parents never forgive, if they never feel the child has offered sufficient atonement, and if they never approve. In this case, the child's anxiety and guilt are continuous, and he or she develops a feeling of constant failure and rejection, may even give up trying to please, and may become completely antisocial or incorrigible. This is why disapproval needs to be followed by acceptance and reconciliation once more (Rice, 1980).

A spanking is a quick and tangible punishment that rights the balance, since it is payment for wrongdoing. However, since payment has been made there may be no cause for guilt, and there is not as much stimulus to do right the next time. If physical punishment is harsh and cruel, especially if accompanied by parental rejection, it develops immature, hostile, and rebellious persons, just the opposite of what truly socialized, moral persons ought to be.

The most effective discipline utilizes both rewards and appropriate punishment. The parents stimulate moral development by consistently emphasizing what they consider to be right or wrong as they guide their children's behavior. Eventually children internalize (believe and accept both intellectually and emotionally) these messages from their parents. After that, the children's own inner standards will either reward them by allowing them to feel good when they do right or punish them by causing them to feel bad when they do wrong (Forisha and Forisha, 1976, p. 23).

METHODS WITH TEENAGERS

Types of Control

What kind of family discipline or control best meets the needs of adolescents? There are really four patterns of family control: autocratic, permissive, erratic, and democratic. These may be described as follows:

Autocratic or authoritarian control is where the parents make decisions relating to their teenager.

Permissive control is where the teenager has more control and influence in making decisions than do the parents.

Erratic control is inconsistent—sometimes authoritarian, sometimes democratic, sometimes permissive.

Democratic control is where decisions are made jointly by parents and their teenager (Rice, 1978, p. 416). What effect does each method of control have on teenagers?

Autocratic. Autocratic control usually produces a combination of rebellion and dependency. Teenagers are taught to be submissive, to obey, and to be dependent upon parents for decisions and guidance. They are expected to follow their parents' wishes without question, so they never get a chance to decide things for themselves. As a result, they tend to show less initiative and autonomy and are less self-motivated.

The meeker ones are cowed by such methods; the more rebellious become more hostile, deeply resenting their parents' domination. If parental discipline is harsh and unfair, and administered coldly without love or affection, teenagers become insensitive, uncaring, hostile, rebellious, cruel persons. Instead of teaching adolescents to care about others, it deadens their sensitivities, so that they learn to fear and hate others but no longer care about them or want to please them. When the threat of external punishment is removed, they are antisocial people. Many criminal types fit this description.

What about physical punishment such as a spanking? As far as I am concerned, it is out—especially with teenagers. It is humiliating and builds resentment and anger, so it doesn't really solve any problems. Other methods, such as verbal reasoning or the restricting of privileges, are far more effective in achieving the desired results.

One midnight I received a phone call from a distraught mother whose husband had punched her sixteen-year-old boy in the face with his fists because the boy came home late. The son ran off afterward. My talks with the father were of no avail. He felt he was justified in beating up his son. "It's a father's duty to teach his son to mind" was his attitude. Yet, all the father had succeeded in doing was to drive his son out of the house, and to convince him that the father was a cruel person. In addition, the father had set a negative example of cruelty and violence.

Permissive. The exact opposite of autocratic discipline is extreme permissiveness. In this type of home, adolescents receive little guidance and direction and few restrictions from parents, and are expected to decide things for themselves. Such permissiveness retards socialization and moral development, since teenagers get no help in developing inner controls. Without some external authority, children remain amoral. Adolescents want and need some parental guidance. Without it, they become spoiled, pampered persons who are ill prepared to accept frustrations or responsibility or to show proper regard for others. They often become "spoiled brats" who are domineering, self-centered, and selfish and who are disliked by others for their lack of consideration. They also get into trouble with others who don't pamper them the way their parents have done. Often, without definite guidelines, they become insecure, disoriented, and uncertain and may end up blaming their parents for not guiding them. If they interpret the lack of parental control as lack of interest, or as rejection, they may become resentful of their parents. Lax discipline, rejection, and lack of parental control have been closely associated with delinquency (Rice, 1978, p. 417).

Erratic. Inconsistent parental control also has a negative effect upon adolescents. They become confused and insecure, lacking clear, definite guidelines. Such youths often evince delinquent behavior. One researcher found that 49 percent of youths who reported that their mothers "very often" failed to follow through on threatened punishment were in the "most delinquent" category (Nye, 1958). Also, when parents differ in their exercise of authority, adolescents show more rebellion against both parents and less self-control.

It is important that discipline be kept consistent "intra-parent" (with one parent) and "interparent" (between two parents). Erratic parental expectations lead to poor moral learning, anxiety, confusion, instability, and disobedience. In fact, lack of consistency is most common in families of "amoral" children. Youths who are at this immature level of moral development seldom experience consistent moral standards at home. They are unlikely either to be rewarded for moral behavior or to be punished consistently for disobedience. The combination of a harsh, restrictive father and an overindulgent, lenient mother is inconsistent and especially damaging (Bandura and Walters, 1959).

Democratic. The democratic home has the most positive effect upon adolescents. This type of control expresses parental concern by giving some guidance, but it encourages individual responsibility, decision-making, initiative, and autonomy. Adolescents are involved in making their own decisions while listening to and discussing the reasoned explanations of parents. Adolescents are encouraged to gradually detach themselves from the family. As a result, the home atmosphere is likely to be one of respect, appreciation, warmth, and acceptance. It is in this type of home that warmth, fairness, and consistency of discipline are associated with conforming, trouble-free, nondelinquent behavior for both boys and girls (Rice, 1978, p. 417).

IMPORTANT PRINCIPLES

Clear Explanations

Effective discipline begins with clear explanations of what is required. This means parents have to sort out in their own minds what is important to them. They have to agree between them, and then work out clear requirements in discussion with their teenagers. Once appropriate behavior is discussed, parents have to follow up to check on progress and compliance. One boy remarked, "When my parents ask me to do something, they never check up to see whether I've done it or not." Why do it if parents are not concerned enough to notice?

Enforcement

Parents do have to avoid negative verbal techniques such as belittling and nagging, however. Reasoning or praise used to correct or reinforce behavior enhances learning. The most effective discipline is that which assures compliance. Let us suppose that a teenager has agreed to mow his grandmother's lawn once a week. Enforcement requires that parents check to see if the promise has been kept, and that they follow up to correct insufficiencies. If, for example, the lawn has not been mowed, the best discipline would require that it be done before the teenager goes out. In case of repeated infractions, a penalty would be assigned, such as scrubbing the front porch in addition. If there isn't time for immediate enforcement because of school, the yard and front porch may be left as they are, and the teenager instructed to come home as soon as possible after school to do the necessary chores. This type of discipline is far more effective than grounding the adolescent while leaving the chores undone. Some teenagers are willing to suffer all kinds of penalties and still not do the work. In other words, the discipline is ineffective because it has not trained them to do what is required to be done.

Consequences

Parents have to be willing to let their teenagers assume responsibilities and suffer the consequences if such are not carried out. Some parents defend their teenagers and stand up for them no matter what they do. I heard one girl remark: "Chief———(meaning the police chief) is afraid of my father. He knows if he arrests me, he'll get in plenty of trouble." This is a terrible attitude to develop in young people. Yet some have learned that no matter what they do they will not get into trouble, because their parents will bail them out. I know one boy who totaled three new cars before his father finally refused to buy him another. Each time, the boy left the car after he wrecked it, and later told the police that he had not been driving it and that the car had been stolen. The father knew differently, but he supported his son in his lies. Such misguided "help" is completely detrimental to the development of moral, adult behavior. If their teenagers get into trouble, certainly parents need to help them get legal assistance or other aid as required. But parents also have to let them know that they are going to have to suffer the consequences of their own actions.

Suppose a teenager is given a 35-dollar fine for speeding. As far as I am concerned, it is the young person who is responsible for paying the fine, not the parents. How about the adolescent who misses school or work because of overindulgence the night before, and then wants the parents to make up excuses? My feeling is that the best thing parents can do is stay out of the situation and let teenagers suffer their own consequences.

This does not mean I believe that parents should let teenagers get into trouble if parents can avoid it. But if parents have done everything they can to help teenagers understand the folly of their proposed actions, and if the youths still insist on going ahead, then they are responsible, not the parents. I know one teenage girl who bore three babies out of wedlock. Each time, she took the baby home to her mother to take care of it. If the girl is going to have babies, then let her be responsible for taking care of them. There are consequences to actions, and moral maturity requires this awareness.

Individual

Whatever disciplinary methods parents use should be geared to the individual. Some supersensitive teenagers are crushed by only a sharp word. Others require stricter measures. Some are quite rebellious and must be handled with kid gloves. Others are easygoing and cooperative and do not readily take offense. Some youths respond better to some rewards than to others. For example, some youths are not competitive and do not respond well to prizes and special recognition. Other rewards must be used if they are to be motivated at all. In complex situations, particular and direct reinforcement of desired behavior often does not work (Forisha and Forisha, 1976, p. 60). In such cases, parents may have to change their approach entirely. This is one reason why child-rearing is such a humbling experience. Valuable lessons learned in rearing one child may be useless in rearing the next one. Individual teenagers have different feelings, needs, and personalities, so parents have to be flexible and deal with each person on an individual basis.

Fair and Reasonable

Whatever discipline is used must be fair and reasonable. Parents who overreact by instituting long-term, strict punishments only build resentment, stimulate their teenagers to disobey, and make it harder for themselves to keep their word. For example, one father told his daughter that she couldn't go out on weekends for the remaining three months of the school term because she came in a half hour later than she was supposed to. Restriction for a weekend or two would have been sufficient punishment to remind the daughter to keep her word. The unnecessarily severe punishment risked making her so resentful that the father-

daughter relationship would be strained over a long period of time.

Some parents threaten but never follow through. This
only serves to undermine their authority and to encourage
teenagers to ignore their wishes. One of the hardest things
about disciplining is to know when to apply pressure and
when to ease up. The best guide is probably one's own
child. Discipline that is used too often loses its effective-
ness because children get so used to it that they virtually
ignore it.

Feelings

One of the most important considerations is how parents and their teenagers feel about one another. Discipline is easier and more effective within the context of a
warm, loving relationship. Teenagers certainly are more
likely to follow parents when they love and admire them
than when the opposite relationship exists. This is why the
particular methods of discipline that are used are even less
important than the overall relationship. Are teens and
parents really warm and affectionate toward each other?
Do they admire each other? Do they always try to show
respect for each other? Do they try to understand each
other? Do they strive to please and to abide by each
other's wishes? If the answer to these questions is "yes,"
then most problems that arise can be solved somehow.

Example

I cannot overestimate the importance of setting a good
example in influencing adolescent behavior. One parent
said: "Figure out what kind of persons you want your
children to become, be that yourself, and they will be like
you when they grow up" (Rice, 1980). This is more likely
to happen if children are in close contact with their par-

ents and if they admire their parents and want to be like them. Sometimes parents exhibit the kind of character and behavior that children dislike, so that the children reject the parents' image and resolve *not* to be like them. Even then, it is hard for the children to break away completely from the parents' influence and not to adopt some parental characteristics, even though these may be negative. In one thirty-year study of adults who as children had been referred to a clinic because of antisocial behavior, the father's antisocial behavior was shown to be the most significant factor that could have been used in predicting the antisocial behavior of these individuals (Robins, 1966).

A more complete discussion of the importance of setting a good example is found in the next chapter.

7

By Way of Example

Show yourself in all respects a model of good deeds, and in
your teaching show integrity, gravity, and sound speech
that cannot be censured. (Titus 2:7, 8)

NEED FOR LIVING EXAMPLES

Christian Leaders

One of the important emphases in this letter to Titus is
the need to set a good example. Elders of the church are
to be "blameless." A bishop "must not be arrogant or
quick-tempered or a drunkard or violent or greedy for
gain, but hospitable, a lover of goodness, master of himself,
upright, holy, and self-controlled" (Titus 1:7, 8). Older
men are to be "temperate, serious, sensible, sound in faith,
in love, and in steadfastness" (Titus 2:2). Older women
likewise are "to be reverent in behavior, not to be slander-
ers or slaves to drink; they are to teach what is good, and
so train the young women to love their husbands and
children, to be sensible, chaste, domestic, kind, and submissive to their husbands, that the word of God may not
be discredited" (Titus 2:3–5).

In these words, all Christians are being admonished to

show by their lives that they know God and that he is working out his salvation in them. Too many persons "profess to know God, but they deny him by their deeds" (Titus 1:16).

If children and youths are to be moral persons, they need living examples. It is not enough for adults to urge, "Do as I say, not as I do." Such an admonition is generally ineffectual. This fact has been demonstrated in many ways.

Peers

One experiment was conducted with nursery school children who alternated as customer and storekeeper in a toy-store situation. For some children a peer model was instructed to tell the children that on completion of the game they could take a single piece of candy, whereupon the peer model took three pieces. Other children were confronted with a peer model who repeated the instruction to take one piece of candy and then himself took only one. After the peer model left the room, the children who had watched the peer model who took three pieces took more pieces of candy more often than did the children who had seen the peer model who took only one piece. Furthermore, the children who took more than one piece evidenced guilt and conflict and sometimes tried to conceal the act (Bandura and Walters, 1963, p. 176).

Parents

Another researcher made a study of influential factors in the lives of partially committed versus fully committed civil rights workers. He found that the most fully committed workers had dominant parents who were quite altruistic in their own behavior. The workers had modeled their own lives after them. The partially committed workers were socialized by parents who often demonstrated inconsistent behavior, usually advocating moral and altruistic behavior but not always practicing it themselves. The consistently altruistic model was missing and these young peoples' commitment to altruistic causes was only partially realized (Rosenhan, 1969).

Most parents today are concerned about the increasing use of drugs among youths. It has been found that adolescents who use marijuana are more likely to have parents who drink excessively or who use psychotropic drugs (Tec, 1970, 1974). Similarly, adolescents are more likely to start and to continue smoking if their parents smoke (Horn, 1959). Drinking patterns among adolescents also generally follow the adult models in their communities. Parents who drink are more likely to have adolescents who drink; parents who do not drink are more likely to have youths who do not drink (Bacon and Jones, 1968).

Youths say they want parents who

> "Practice what they preach"
> "Set a good example for us to follow"
> "Follow the same principles they try to teach us"
> (Rice, 1978, p. 418)

By being moral themselves, parents are able to offer a positive role model for their young people to follow.

WORDS MADE FLESH

Abstractions

Many religious principles, such as love, for example, are vague and abstract concepts, but when children experience love in other persons, they don't have to be *told* about love, they *know* it because they see and feel it. The same is true regarding other moral virtues, such as truthfulness, kindness, honesty, humility. These are only words that symbolize important realities, but when these words become flesh, when they become real in human personalities, their meaning is unmistakable and clear.

God's Truths

Actually, this was God's way of revealing great truths about himself. In Christ, the thoughts of God became real so that "the Word became flesh and dwelt among us, full of grace and truth; we have beheld his glory, glory as of the only Son from the Father" (John 1:14). People no longer had to wonder about God; they had seen him and talked with him. They now had a living example of what he was like and the kind of person he wanted them to become.

A businessman was walking in Central Park in New York City when he saw a shabbily dressed man sitting on a park bench looking dejected. He walked over and sat down.

"What seems to be the matter?" he inquired.

"My sister who lives in Iowa is very sick, and I'd like to go to see her, but I don't know how I can get there." The man explained that his sister was dying of cancer, that he had not seen her for several years, and that he wished he could visit her before she died.

The businessman had met many panhandlers before, but there was something different about this man. The man seemed so sincere, the story must be true. He took the man to the nearest train station, bought him a ticket, and saw him off on the train. The man shook his hand, and with tears in his eyes thanked him. "You're a good man," he said. "You remind me of Jesus Christ on earth." Once more, the Word had become flesh and one man found God in another because God lived in him—full of grace and truth.

DIFFERENT MODELS

Status

There are a number of different factors that influence the model which children and young people choose. One factor is the status of the model. Youths are likely to choose models who are successful, prestigious, or in other ways of high status. This fact has far-reaching implications. Our society gives high status to movie stars, television personalities, and public officials. Youths may ascribe high status to members of rock groups or to recording stars. Unfortunately, many times these persons are not models of morality. In fact, some are just the opposite. When elected officials such as the President or the Vice-President of the United States present images of immorality, and when other adults in our society condone their actions, young people become cynical because those who are supposed to be superior examples of morality have let them down.

Authority and Power

Another factor that influences the choice of model is the authority and power of the model. Youths are more likely to follow those who are recognized authorities: a clergyman, a teacher, a professional person. One of the reasons that youths sometimes reject the words of their parents is that they doubt the ability of their parents to speak authoritatively about particular things.

Unpunished Example

Adolescents are also more likely to follow the negative example of an adult who does something wrong and gets away with it than they are to follow the example of an adult who does something wrong and is punished. A policeman who takes bribes or enforces the law prejudicially and gets away with it presents a negative model to youths, who figure that if a police officer can break the law, they ought to be able to do it too. Similarly, children are more likely to model themselves after parents who exhibit law-breaking behavior and don't get caught or punished (Forisha and Forisha, 1976, p. 58). This is why it is important that immoral actions not go unnoticed or unpunished. If they do, additional persons will be stimulated to do likewise.

Occupations

Occupations are important factors in youths' choice of models. They choose models whose occupations are glamorous, or adventurous, or which bring them fame, wealth, travel, independence, or power. Boys may seek models who are known for their masculinity as represented by their he-man appearance, by their athletic skill and prowess, or by their success and power. One boy says: "The person I would most like to be is . . . a footballer (who) has thrilled millions of people throughout the world" (Eppel and Eppel, 1966, p. 142). Another boy says: "The person I would like to be would be a famous singer." Still another admits: "I would like to be a millionaire . . . and own chains of different stores. . . . I'd wear fine clothes and have at least 3 cars. I would have my own airplane, yacht, and country estate, where I would hold parties for my friends and relations" (p. 143).

Girls may seek models who are glamorous film stars, singers, or fashion designers. One girl says: "The person I would most like to be is a film actress, Leslie Caron. I think she has everything, gorgeous eyes, hair and features, also a sweet figure and personality" (Eppel and Eppel, 1966, p. 144). Another girl fantasizes: "I would like to be a great fashion designer with a glamorous fashion house in all the capitals of the world. I would design the most beautiful dress one could ever wish to see and wear" (p. 144).

Humanitarianism and Altruism

There is a significant minority of young people who want to model their lives after persons who are known for their great humanitarianism or altruism, or even just for simple goodness. A seventeen-year-old girl wrote: "If I really had to choose someone, I think I would choose my mother. She is very kind and always helps anyone who needs it. She is the dearest person in the world. I would like to be like her, more than anyone else" (Eppel and Eppel, 1966, p. 132). Another seventeen-year-old girl reveals her altruism: "I think I should like to be someone who helps others in trouble. Maybe a nurse caring for the sick, or relief helper to give people courage, in times when all hope has gone" (p. 145).

One of the ways of influencing young people to express moral values through their occupations is by bringing them into contact with persons they can admire and emulate. The lives of many youths have been changed by assisting clergymen, congressmen, schoolteachers, doctors, nurses, or business people. By providing worthy role models for their youths, parents can stimulate young people to follow in their footsteps.

8
Learning Through Doing

THE ROLE OF EXPERIENCE

One of the best ways to encourage moral growth and development in children is to provide opportunities to learn through doing. "Experience is the best teacher," as we say, and "Practice makes perfect."

Physical Skills

Actually, children learn most things through experience. When a baby is learning to walk, her parents will put her on a rug and let her move around, begin to crawl, pull and hold herself up, and take her first hesitant steps while holding on to something. The parents may hold on to her to help steady her, but they really need not give her instructions in *how* to walk. All they need do is give her an opportunity to practice and she will learn little by little.

The same process takes place in learning other physical skills such as roller-skating or riding a bicycle. The parents can give a minimum of instructions in bike-riding, but the way children really learn is through practice and experience, by getting on the bike and trying to ride. They fall down frequently in the beginning, but as balance and skill develop, their spills become less frequent and eventually the fine art is mastered.

Intellectual Skills

Intellectual and mental skills may also be developed through practice. The more children read, the greater the facility they develop in reading. The more they hear others speak and the more opportunities they have to talk, the more readily they are able to express themselves.

Social Behavior

Social behavior is also learned behavior—learned primarily through social participation and practice. One good way for children to learn how to get along with others is simply to be with others, to have the chance to share and to learn consideration and cooperation. Parents of young children easily learn the value of nursery school and kindergarten experience in teaching social skills. Even imitative play becomes a means of learning.

> Play may well be called a child's preparation for life. To a child, play is . ... his way of learning.
> Watch a small girl at play, imitating her mother in her household tasks and in the care she gives the baby. Watch a small boy pretending to be his father coming home from the office. As you watch, you are observing the learning process at work. (Cully, 1963, p. 503)

Religious Training

Parents and teachers who understand the value of participation and of doing in learning can use such knowledge in the religious training of children and young people. The best way for a person to develop habits of devotion such as Bible-reading, prayer, and worship is through participation and experience. Children learn to read and use the Bible by doing so. They learn to pray by praying. They develop the habit of going to church and Sunday school by going each Sunday with the family. People who say they can worship God without going to church are right. They can—but do they? Or, they can pray without being in church. Of course—but do they? Most adults as well as children need regularly scheduled times for prayer and worship so that such practices become habitual. They also need opportunities for learning, self-examination, periodic renewal, and dedication. This is why Sunday school, youth fellowship experiences, spiritual retreats, and camp and conference opportunities for young people are especially needed. It gives them a chance to act, to commit themselves anew to Christ and to renew their resolve to follow him. Christian growth takes place through repeated repentance and commitment. People don't become Christian just by talking. They do so by acting, by participating in meaningful experiences that help them to grow in understanding, dedication, and love.

Attitudinal Development

One parent relates how her teenagers came home one day using the slang word "Spik" for Mexican Americans. The parents had never used such language, so it was obvious the youths picked it up from their friends. Then and there the mother decided she wanted to help her adolescents develop more understanding of members of this minority group. The first thing she did was take them to visit a migrant worker camp nearby. The teenagers were appalled by the living conditions, but especially at the long, hard days of work in the fields and the low wages. The mother then asked the teenagers to invite some Mexi-

can-American classmates to their home for a visit and for
supper. Gradually, the adolescents began to get to know
these Mexican Americans as friends. They never called
them "Spiks" again.

METHODS OF DOING

Social Service

Opportunities for social service should be an important
part of the Christian experience of young people. The
annual youth budget canvass in church gives youths a
chance to enlist pledges from one another for the ongoing
work of the church. In so doing, they not only learn to
organize and conduct such a canvass, and to serve their
church, but when this activity is accompanied by an educational program they learn what their church is doing to
help others at home and abroad. One youth group volunteered to pay all the expenses for an orphan child to be
taken care of for one year in a Christian mission. Another
raised money to send to a private home for unwed mothers. Still another sent money to a mission hospital in Africa.
Another contributed toward a scholarship fund to pay college expenses of underprivileged teenagers from the
inner city.

Youths need a chance not only to raise money for worthwhile projects but also to donate their time and talents to
worthy causes. Here are some sample social service projects that can help youths to gain increased understanding
of the problems of other people.

> Do volunteer work in a nursing home. Visit with the
> elderly, read to them, provide transportation for
> ambulatory patients, write letters, go shopping,

take patients for a stroll in a wheelchair.

Work in a Head Start Center. Assist the teacher with the daily supervision of the children, supervise lunchtime or playtime, make toys or large playground equipment, build a play yard, paint the walls of a playroom.

Do volunteer work in the children's ward of a hospital. Read to the children, play with them, supervise creative activity periods.

Do volunteer work in a school for the mentally retarded.

Assist teachers in working with the physically handicapped.

Field Trips

Field trips provide an excellent opportunity to gain insights into people's problems. Here are some suggested field trips:

Visit a resident home for unwed mothers.

Visit the psychiatric ward of a local hospital

Sit in on juvenile court hearings.

Visit an alcohol and/or drug rehabilitation center.

Visit a county jail or a state prison.

Accompany a social worker in calling on low-income families.

I will never forget taking members of a youth group with me one afternoon while making pastoral calls. I called on several parishioners who were sick in the hospital and visited some shut-ins, as well as some low-income mothers who were having an especially hard time. The teenagers were impressed with the poor living conditions of the low-income mothers. Most of the apartments were in disrepair, dirty, and cluttered. The paint was peeling off the walls, the roofs leaked, the furniture was shabby and torn.

"We had no idea that people lived like that" was the most common reaction of the young people. As a result of their visits, these youths decided to raise money to send several children from these low-income families to summer day camp while the mothers were at work.

Creative Activities

Learning experiences may include various creative activities. One junior high class constructed a model of the Temple in Jerusalem, including the Ark of the Covenant and the various interior spaces and furnishings. They made Jewish costumes, including those a priest might wear, and then participated in a Temple service of worship. By actually being a part of the service, they could more fully understand the meaning it would have had to the participants.

Creative activities are primarily a way of communicating. Such activities may include the use of art materials to make posters, dioramas, displays, or exhibits. For example, one group decided to illustrate the Christian teenager's use of time. The group first did a summary among adolescents to determine how they actually divided their time during one week. They published the results in the form of an illustrated circle graph or poster. They then made another poster to show that what they felt was a more Christian division of time.

Posters may be used in several ways. A poster that is used to educate might illustrate the variety of missionary activities overseas. A poster that is used to exhort or urge a group to take a particular action might say: "Go to Church Every Sunday."

Creative activities may include the writing of poems, essays, short stories, and plays. One group wrote a play about a teenage boy who was considered "queer" and who was ridiculed and ostracized because he was "different." The group put on the play and then discussed their attitudes and feelings and what they should do about such social outcasts. The members of another group were each asked to write an essay on "What I Want to Do with My Life." These essays became the springboard for discussions about the ultimate meaning of life and what these young people wanted to do with theirs.

Some youths are musically talented enough to write and play hymns, gospel songs, or religious folk music. Such activities become a fine way of expressing and teaching deep religious feelings and ideas.

Drama

One good way to deal with sensitive social problems or interpersonal relationships is through the use of role-playing. Role-playing is an educational tool in which class members act out the roles, functions, or emotions that people employ knowingly or unknowingly in interpersonal relationships. Role-playing is really impromptu drama in which a situation is presented to a group of young people who have been selected as the actors to play out the scene as they imagine it might have taken place. They make up the words as they go along, and members of the audience later discuss what they have seen and heard and the implications for their own lives. The discussion helps them to gain deeper insights and to achieve appropriate behavior modification. Role-playing may be used to illustrate such things as:

Parent-teen relationships

 Peer influences
 Dating problems
 Speech patterns and habits

Appropriate subjects or situations are almost endless.

Of course, more formal religious drama may be employed. Putting on a major two- or three-act play can be a worthwhile project for any youth group, and if appropriate literature is selected, this can be a valuable means of communicating great moral truths.

VICARIOUS EXPERIENCE

It is impossible and most unwise to try to expose young people to every conceivable type of personal experience through which they might learn important truths. For example, how many parents really want their daughters to get pregnant and to have an abortion or to have a baby out of wedlock so they will learn sexual responsibility? Or, how many want their youths to spend the night in jail to learn not to speed or drive recklessly? While such experiences certainly teach, there are less painful ways of learning the same truths. No parent wants his teenager to go to prison for murder to learn the commandment "You shall not kill."

One way of teaching is to offer vicarious experiences by exposing youths to others who have had the experiences and who are willing to share them. I will never forget taking a group to a resident home for unwed mothers. Just to see and talk to a group of thirty unmarried but pregnant girls, ranging in age from 12 to 23 years, was a most sobering experience.

The controversial television program *Scared Straight* shows the visit of a group of juvenile offenders to a state prison where they are shouted at, threatened, bullied, cursed, and abused by seasoned convicts who have volunteered to try to help these offenders really realize what it is like to be in prison. The purpose, of course, is to scare them with the realities of prison life—with such things as homosexual abuse, for example—so that they will go back to their own communities with a resolve to give up their life of crime. The efforts to scare youthful offenders straight have been partially successful and are now being widely considered by other states. This is really a dramatic use of vicarious or shared experience as a means of moral teaching.

Just recently the police in my own community parked the wreckage of a car by the roadside near the local high school. The car had belonged to a seventeen-year-old boy who wrapped it around a sturdy oak tree when he failed to negotiate a corner at a speed of over 100 miles an hour. The boy was under the influence of drugs when he wiped out his own life so tragically. I know that hundreds of youths went to see the car and were moved by what they saw. This is a positive example of providing vicarious experience through which young people can learn important truths.

Part III
SOCIAL INFLUENCES
AND MORAL GROWTH

9
Peer-Group Influences and Adolescent Behavior

Emotional Need

The need for close friends during adolescence becomes quite intense. Up to this time, children have sought out playmates with whom they could share common interests or activities, but they have not depended upon them primarily for emotional fulfillment. They have looked to their parents for fulfillment of their needs for praise, love, and tenderness. Only if parents have rejected them will they have turned to friends or parent substitutes (Rice, 1978, p. 314).

But after puberty, all this changes. Sexual maturation creates new feelings and the desire for emotional independence, and the adolescent begins to turn to friends for the support formerly given by family members. As they grow older, adolescents desire close, caring relationships with those with whom they can share affection and personal thoughts and concerns. They want friends who will stand beside them and for them in an understanding, loyal way (Rice, 1978, p. 314).

Here are some comments of adolescent boys:

A good friend
   . . . will help you when you're in need of it.
   . . . (is) someone who would do almost anything for you.
   . . . understands your ways as well as his own.
   . . . (is the) best thing in the world to tell your troubles to
and share your happiness with.

(Eppel and Eppel, 1966, pp. 70, 71)

Several adolescent girls made these comments:

A good friend
   . . . is someone who trusts you and believes you and would
do anything for you.
   . . . (is) someone of the same interests and views on life.
   . . . (is) someone whom you love and trust, who takes you
with all your faults.
   . . . is someone who is very dear and cannot be replaced
by earthly belongings.

(Eppel and Eppel, 1966, pp. 71, 72)

Group Participation

Because of their emotional need for friends, adolescents
put a great deal of emphasis on belonging to a group and
on being well liked. They try very hard to become members of a clique or crowd they admire. They are ultrasensi-
tive to criticism and to any indications of rejection, anything that might show that they are not accepted. When
one group of teenagers was asked to name "the people
whose opinion of you matters a great deal to you," 70
percent included one or more of their age mates (Rosen,
1965, p. 84).

One of the ways teenagers have of not being rejected is
that of conforming to group standards of behavior and
trying to be like the members of their group. Each group
has a character of its own: the members have their own
special slang, their own style of dress, their particular interest in certain types of activities. Thus, one group may

be known as "the leading crowd" in school. It is composed of those who come from the "right" families, wear nice clothes, are leaders in activities, are athletes, have nice cars, and make respectable grades. Another group may be known as "toughs." They wear leather jackets and distinctive hairstyles; they are often in trouble with the police, drink and use drugs heavily, create disturbances in school, and pride themselves on their lack of attention to academic matters. When teenagers join a particular group, they have to be as much like other members of their group as possible. If they are not, they are excluded as "queer." They are expected to do what other members of the group do. Thus, the adolescent boy who wants to belong to a juvenile gang of delinquents and has to pull off a robbery to do so is confronted with a peer code that may get him into trouble.

Other writers have referred to the group life of adolescents as herd life. The herd assembles at the local hangout for refreshments and small talk; the herd goes joyriding in the car, or to a drive-in movie or a dance, or to hear a rock group at the local community center. The herd may go on a hayride, skiing, or to the seashore. To be a part of the social scene, one has to join the herd and be with them (Stone and Church, 1958, p. 459).

GROUP INFLUENCES

Influence on Behavior

The implications of all this in relation to moral development and behavior are quite obvious. The kinds of friends that adolescents choose, and the types of groups they join, are crucial in their development and have considerable influence on their behavior. One study found, for example, that the best single indicator of whether or not an adolescent boy showed deviant social behavior was the extent of deviance of the peer group that he went around with (Albrecht et al., 1977, p. 271). One reason is that adolescents do model their behavior after that of friends they admire. One sixteen-year-old English boy commented: "I would like to be like John. He is big and he is a good mate" (Eppel and Eppel, 1966, p. 133). A girl remarked: "I would like to be so many girls in the way they dress, behave and enjoy themselves" (p. 134).

Street Gangs

Another reason the nature of the group is important is that members force one another to do things they wouldn't do otherwise. Some juvenile street gangs hold nearly absolute control over the behavior of individual members. One investigation of juvenile street gangs in Philadelphia showed that members were expected to get drunk, fight, get and hide a weapon, cause trouble at school and in the neighborhood, call the police names, break up parties, destroy public property, and mark or spray paint on walls. The violent nature of these gangs is shown by the fact that 25 percent of individual members were forced to shoot at someone, 22 percent were forced to stab or injure someone, 27 percent were forced to steal, and 7 percent were forced to take heroin and 7 percent to take speed (Friedman et al., 1976). These gangs held life-and-death power over others and were a direct challenge to the authority of parents, police, community leaders, and school officials. Members were forced to submit to the gang's decisions or face personally destructive consequences.

Group Pressures

Of course, not all adolescent groups are delinquent, destructive, or a threat to the community. But even socially accepted groups do put pressure on other members to behave in ways they wouldn't if by themselves. It takes fairly secure, independent persons to resist group pressures and only to do what they as individuals really want to do and what they consider right to do. One girl commented:

> When I was in high school, I used to smoke pot, try speed, drink too much, and do all of the other things everybody else was doing. I'm not into those things any longer. That's kid stuff. I really don't like drugs, so I decided I was going to do what I wanted, and if someone didn't like it, they could go out with someone else. I've found that I still have a few good friends. A lot of kids are like I am, but they won't stand up for themselves until somebody like me comes along and shows them they can be different and still be accepted—at least by someone.

Conformity

Studies of adolescents indicate that younger adolescents tend to go along with the crowd more than do older teenagers. The tendency to conform usually increases to about age 13 for girls and age 15 for boys, and then declines (Costanzo and Shaw, 1966). Also, teenagers who have good relationships with their parents show fewer tendencies to conform to peer demands than do adolescents who come from troubled homes. Thus, it is those who aren't getting along at home who are more likely to spend increased time with peers, and to come under their influence. One boy commented, "When I was growing up, all my parents did was fight, so I would go out of the house all the time to be with my gang." Also, adolescents who attend church

and who do well in school are less likely to be influenced
negatively by their peers.

IMPLICATIONS FOR PARENTS

Attitudes Toward Unsuitable Friends

These facts have important implications for parents.
One thing that troubles parents is what to do about friends
whom they consider undesirable. One mother writes:

> We are becoming concerned because of the type of friends
> our son is going around with. They seem rather wild. They
> don't seem to have much ambition; they drink too much,
> have too much money and freedom, and unlimited use of
> cars. Should we forbid our son from seeing them?

My own answer is that I would not forbid the son to see
them, but I would let him know how I felt and why I was
concerned. Most teenagers feel they should have the right
to choose their own friends. If the parents of this youth
forbid contacts, they are encouraging their son to be resentful and rebellious and to sneak behind their back.
However, if the parents do nothing, then they are not
fulfilling their responsibilities to try to guide and influence. One reasonable approach would be for the parents
to discuss their concerns, the reasons for their worry, and
to indicate that they prefer that their son keep other company. At the same time, the parents have to make it clear
that the decision must be the son's and that he is responsible for his behavior. It does help if parents explain some
of the pitfalls and dangers of wrong company, and try to
get their children to see that every person is known partly
by the company he or she keeps.

One of the handicaps that parents are under is that they
aren't always good judges of the basic character, behavior,

and morals of teenagers whom they know only superficially. Certainly, parents can't tell by looks, or by family background, or even by the way youths behave in their presence. Some youths whom parents may feel are "very nice kids" because they come from well-to-do families may be real delinquents when adults are not around. A girl who seems so polite may be promiscuous sexually. A boy who has nice clothes may enjoy "ripping off" stores just for kicks. Actually, only teenagers know who does what. They know which kids are wild and delinquent and which are not.

But adolescents are also quite inexperienced and naive about some things—including the serious implications of going with others who may get them into trouble. "Oh, he's a nice guy" is often the comment that teenagers make about a boy who actually gets into a lot of trouble. Youths hesitate to condemn anybody. But parents can help their own youngsters see that they have to be concerned about their own reputation and behavior—and that they ought not to jeopardize either by going with the wrong type of people.

Membership in Youth Organizations

One answer is for parents to encourage membership in youth groups and organizations that are likely to exert a positive influence.

Here is only a partial listing of some of the more common organizations (Hanson and Carlson, 1972):

Outdoor-oriented Agencies
  Boy Scouts of America
  Girl Scouts of the U.S.A.
  American Youth Hostels

Religious-oriented Organizations

Young Men's Christian Association (YMCA)
Young Women's Christian Association (YWCA)
Young Men's Hebrew Association (YMHA)
Young Women's Hebrew Association (YWHA)
Jewish Community Centers
B'nai B'rith Youth Organization
Three Jewish youth groups associated with synagogues:
  National Federation of Temple Youth (Reform)
  United Synagogue Youth (Conservative)
  National Council of Young Israel (Orthodox)
Salvation Army youth programs:
  Girl Guards—10 to 13 years
  Senior Guards—Girls 14 to 18
Protestant denominational youth programs
Youth for Christ
Catholic Youth Organization (CYO)
American Youth Foundation

Vocationally-oriented Organizations
4-H Clubs
Future Farmers of America
Junior Achievement
Future Scientists of America
Candy-Stripers

Organizations Serving the Disadvantaged
Boys' Clubs of America
Girls' Clubs of America
Police Athletic League
Big Brothers of America

Other Organizations
Junior Red Cross
American Legion and American Legion Auxiliary Corps
  Boys' State and Boys' Nation
  Girls' State and Girls' Nation
Masonic Youth Organizations
  Rainbow Girls
  Demolay
National Honor Society
Little League

Certainly, there is no shortage of organizations for young people. It remains for parents and youth leaders to influence young people to join organizations that will exert the most positive influence on their lives.

10
Television, Movies, and Social Values

TELEVISION VIEWING BEHAVIOR

Exposure

It is estimated that by the time they have graduated from high school most children have watched about 20,-000 hours of television. This may be compared with 11,000 hours spent in the school classroom and about 400 hours in religious education, assuming they have attended church or Sunday school one hour every other week for sixteen years (Elder, 1976, p. 80; Rice, 1978, p. 530).

It is not difficult to see that, measured simply in terms of total exposure, television can have a far greater impact upon children than either school or church. Recent long-term studies have indicated that the influence of television and peer groups on children has been increasing, while parental and family influence on the socialization of children is steadily decreasing (Bronfenbrenner, 1970).

It behooves us to know of the potential effects of this powerful and omnipresent source of influence. It would be wrong to assume, from the outset, that all the effects of television are necessarily bad—or good. But it could be folly to "ignore" the possible effects and to allow this massive intrusion into the daily lives of children without at least questioning its impact. (Bronfenbrenner, 1970)

Research shows that the number of hours spent in television-viewing increases each year up until somewhere between 9 and 13 years of age, after which it declines somewhat during high school (Rubin, 1977). It is significant that the greatest amount of viewing time is spent during the most formative school years. Teenagers spend more time out of the house and doing other things, and so watch less television.

Other Factors

There do seem to be considerable differences in viewing habits, not only because of age but also because of other factors. Children from low-income and minority-group families tend to watch more television than do those from middle-class families. One researcher found that black children in the first, second, and third grades in New Orleans, Louisiana, watched television 3.1 hours each weekday and 4.2 hours a day on Saturday and Sunday. Saturday morning was the most popular time with 52 percent watching then. Next in popularity was the time after school with 45 percent, and after dinner with 23 percent (Donohue, 1975, p. 158). A study of emotionally disturbed adolescents between the ages of 13 and 18 at a state mental hospital in Louisiana revealed that the average patient watched television 8½ to 9 hours a day! After supper, during adult television hours, was the most popular viewing time for these teenagers.

Why Watch?

When another group, made up of 9-, 13-, and 17-year-olds, were asked *why* they watched television, the following percentages gave their reasons.

> 52%—To learn about things in the world, about things I don't learn in school, to learn how to do things, to learn about myself, about what could happen to me, and how other people deal with the same problems I have.
>
> 19%—To pass the time when I have nothing to do, to give me something to do, because it's a habit and I like to watch it.
>
> 10%—For companionship, so I won't be lonely when there's no one to talk to or play with.
>
> 8%—To forget about school, homework, the family, or to get away from what I'm doing.
>
> 6%—For arousal, excitement, because it's thrilling, it stirs me up.
>
> 5%—For relaxation, it calms me down, it's a pleasant rest.
>
> (Rubin, 1977)

In spite of the fact that over half of these youths said they watched television to learn, the study showed that few children watched news and public affairs programs, and even fewer showed a preference for children's educational programs. Entertainment, principally in the form of comedies and adventure-drama programs, was the favored program content across all three age groups (Rubin, 1977, p. 361).

EFFECTS ON CHILDREN AND YOUTHS

Commercials

The real question about commercials is: What is their effect on these young viewers? More than one fourth of total viewing time is spent on commercials. One writer estimates that today's children are exposed to more than 350,000 commercial messages before they graduate from high school (Looney, 1971). We can only guess at the net effects of these messages. Many thinking persons feel that television commercials sometimes arouse anxieties and feelings of insecurity in children (Culley et al., 1976). We do know that advertising sells, and that children pressure their parents to buy toys, cereals, candies, and other items they see advertised on television. Most experts agree that there ought to be much closer supervision of commercial advertising aimed at children (Culley et al., 1976).

Violence

Public concern over the content of television has focused on the effect on children and youths of watching so much violence. By the time children are age 14 and in the eighth grade, they will have watched 18,000 human beings killed on television and will have witnessed violent assaults on thousands more (Looney, 1971). A Michigan State University study showed that children are more likely to see violence on television on Saturday morning than during the weeknight "family hour," and that violence was almost twice as high on Saturday morning as on prime time. This study also said that the 8–9 P.M. family hour had about the same number of violent acts as the next two hours, which had been designated adult-show hours ("TV Study," 1977).

The real question remains: What effect does television violence have on the moral behavior of children and youths? A report of the United States Surgeon General's advisory committee on television and children's aggressions indicates that there is no causal relationship between television programs on which violence is depicted and aggressive behavior in children (U.S. Surgeon General, 1972). However, Liebert and Neale, two social scientists who were members of the committee, indicated their dissatisfaction with the report. They believed the data were distorted and in some cases misinterpreted in arriving at compromises in writing the report. They quote from the report:

> As matters now stand, the weight of the experimental evidence from the present series of studies, as well as from prior research, suggests that viewing filmed violence has an observable effect on some children in the direction of increasing their aggressive behavior.... On the basis of these findings, and taking into account their variety and their inconsistencies, we can tentatively conclude that there is a modest relationship between exposure to television violence and aggressive behavior or tendencies, as the latter are defined in the studies at hand. (U.S. Surgeon General, 1972, pp. 109, 178)

According to Liebert and Neale (1972), the data showed remarkable breadth and showed that any child from a normal background may respond to television by behaving somewhat more aggressively. They quote further from two other studies:

> Our research shows that among boys and girls at two grade levels (junior high and senior high) the more the child watches violent television fare, the more aggressive he is likely to be. . . . A substantial component (of aggressive behavior at age 19) can be predicted better by the amount of television violence which the child watched in the third grade than by any other causal variable measured, and reinforces the contention that there is a cause-and-effect relation between the violence content of television and overt aggressive behavior. (Liebert and Neale, 1972)

Most of the research on the relationship between television violence and aggression in children and adolescents supports this finding that there is a definite correlation. Bandura and others showed that when children watched unusually aggressive behavior in a real-life model or a model in a film or in a cartoon, many of the children's responses were accurate imitations of the aggressive acts of the model, although the cartoon aggressive model elicited less precise imitation (Bandura, Ross, and Ross, 1963). Walters produced similar findings with high school students, young women, and male hospital attendants (Bandura and Walters, 1959). This research has led to much concern about the dangers of children and adolescents watching aggressive behavior on television screens, since "exposure to filmed aggression heightens aggressive reactions" (Bandura, Ross, and Ross, 1963, p. 9).

Children Most Affected

An additional problem arises because children and youths who need the most positive influences are the ones who watch the most television and are the most affected by its violence. Thus, youths who have the most trouble identifying with parents are the very ones who most identify with favorite television characters who engage in violence and antisocial behavior (Donohue, 1977, p. 343). Adolescents who perform poorly in school watch considerably more violent television, are more likely to approve of aggression, and are generally more likely to behave aggressively (Cater and Strickland, 1975, p. 52). Lower-class children find the violence they see on television more acceptable than do middle-class children. More males than females prefer violent programs. Younger children report more violent responses than do older children (Donohue, 1975).

Furthermore, children learn novel and different acts of violence from watching television, acts that they would not have thought of by themselves. The more children are exposed to media violence, the more emotionally insensitive they become to it and the more they accept it as "normal" behavior (Pastore, 1975). And there is no objective evidence that television violence has a cathartic effect by draining off aggressive energy harmlessly (Magnuson, 1975).

EFFECTS ON OTHER MORAL VALUES AND BEHAVIOR

Six Social Values

Television violence increases aggressiveness in children, but just as importantly, television also influences other moral values and behavior. LeMasters lists six predominant values portrayed by the media that are in conflict with those of most parents attempting to prepare their children for the future.

1. *Sex:* Usually presented in movies and TV on a physical level, both visually and verbally, yet is presented to the viewers as "love."

2. *Violence:* By age 14 the average American child has seen 18,000 human beings killed on TV.

3. *The Idealization of Immaturity:* Idols are not Abraham Lincoln, but are often as juvenile and immature as is the viewer, and seemed to have gained "early wealth and fame ... with a little talent and beauty and a hard-driving agent."

4. *Materialism:* The implication is that happiness comes with success, and success comes with houses, cars, and rugs ... and it all seems free—on the easy credit plan.

5. *Hedonism:* Exposure to an unreal world to which one can easily escape ... and be entertained.

6. *Commercialism of the media.*

(LeMasters, 1974)

The corresponding parental values on these issues are, of course, sexual restraint (and a linkage of sex with love); lifetime monogamy; avoidance of violence; developing responsibility, industry, and maturity; and planning for the future as opposed to now and the enjoyment of it (Gunter and Moore, 1975). To be sure, some parents by their behavior and example represent many of the negative values of which LeMasters speaks. His findings cannot be applied to all television programs or to all parents, but part of what he says is true (Rice, 1978, p. 532).

Television advertising has also been criticized for portraying superficial views of social and personal problems and their solution. Problems of romance, engagement, marriage, child-rearing, employment, and neighborhood relations can all be solved by chemical means. Use a particular headache remedy, nasal spray, deodorant, or toothpaste and find happiness (Gunter and Moore, 1975).

While daytime soap operas are written and produced for housewives, they are watched by thousands of teenagers during afterschool hours. One analysis of 600 hours of eight soap operas revealed the following:

1. The families are all upper middle class with expensive tastes, comfortable or lavish homes, housekeepers and nurses for the children, expensive wardrobes and vacations. No primary male characters have working class occupations. Fifty percent are either physicians or lawyers.

2. The women are primarily affluent housewives who do their own housework because they "love it." Only eight out of fifty-seven female characters are professional. Nineteen are either clericals, domestics, or shopowners. Thus, female roles are stereotyped.

3. The characters are constantly confronted with problems, rape (often by relatives), whether or not to have an abortion, infertility and whether or not to employ artificial insemination, genetic defects, illegitimacy, divorce, death,

extramarital lovers, drug addiction, juvenile delinquency, social drinking and alcoholism, illnesses and operations, and mental illness. Certainly, the social value of these images that are presented to millions of viewers must be questioned. (Ramsdell, 1973)

Postive Values

The most important thing is that television can be used to emphasize positive values such as

work	self-control	appreciation
helping	resistance	for others
sharing	to temptation	consideration
courage	self-worth	kindness
persistence	well-being	unselfishness
thrift	affection and love	concern

Yet these values are seldom exemplified or encouraged. Youths *do* model their behavior after television and screen personalities, actors, and actresses. But what if there aren't enough prosocial behavior models presented to them? One study showed that children were likely to be more inclined to share after watching a television program in which a child was seen to be generous (Liebert et al., 1973, p. 90). There is evidence to show that television can be used to strengthen positive values such as courage. Two researchers used a television model to play with dogs while children who were afraid of dogs watched. It was found that the fear of dogs was reduced greatly after viewing the television model (Liebert et al., 1973, p. 93).

The Place of Television

Elder summarizes the feelings of most of us concerning our role as adults and the place of television in our lives.

Television is here to stay. Parents, children's workers, and the public in general need to place sufficient pressure on the television networks' management and producers to gain positive results in television programs. Television can never take the place of sincere human interaction. Children's values are caught and taught at home, at church, and by society.

[But] television can indeed be a tool for learning. Television can be used to reinforce values acceptable to society as a whole. In our use of television, we need to be careful not to underestimate its power and influence or overestimate its potentialities. (Elder, 1976, pp. 87, 88)

11
The Schools
and Moral Education

THE CONTROVERSIAL ROLE OF THE PUBLIC SCHOOLS

What role should the public schools play in moral education? Over the years, this question has been answered in a variety of ways. Traditionally, the public schools were given the responsibility of teaching moral values. Thus Dewey stated that "formation of character is the end of education" (Dewey, 1911, p. 569). Years later Allport wrote:

> If the school does not teach values, it will have the effect of denying them. If the child at school never hears a mention of honesty, modesty, charity, or reverence, he will be persuaded that, like many of his parents' ideas, they are simply old hat. . . . If the school, which to the child represents the larger outside world, is silent on values, the child will repudiate more quickly the lessons learned at home. He will also be thrown into peer values more completely, with their emphasis on the hedonism of teen-age parties or the destructiveness of gangs. He will also be more at the mercy of the sensate values, peddled by movies, TV and disk jockeys. (Allport, 1961, p. 215)

Allport felt that teachers should reflect those values arising from the whole of our American ethics, particularly as

144

found in the "American Creed" and based on Judeo-Christian ethics.

Other writers have emphasized the need to avoid sectarian religion but nevertheless to ground ethical teachings in the fundamental beliefs of Judeo-Christian religion. Thus in 1924 a Committee on Character Education gave this report to the convention of the National Education Association:

> Many centuries of human experience have led to a consensus of opinion among enlightened peoples that the goal of human development is to be realized through love of God and love of fellow men. Love of God is attested through love of fellow men, and love of fellow men is attested through service. As conceived by all enlightened peoples, love of God and fellow men includes belief in moral standards, in the intrinsic value of the moral life and of personality, compared with which all other values are but relative. (Committee on Character Education, 1924)

Precisely because America was considered a Christian nation, the public school inculcated Christian moral principles while at the same time ignoring controversial theological doctrines. The instrument through which children were instructed in this nondenominational Christianity was the Bible, read without note or comment. The Bible was read "because it breathes God's law and presents illustrious examples of conduct, above all that of Jesus Christ" (McCluskey, 1958, p. 70). No true Christian, regardless of doctrinal confession, questioned its positive influence, reverent tone, and literary excellence. The Scriptures—inevitably the Protestant King James Version—embodied the precepts necessary to transform an impressionable and pliable child into a morally mature and democratic adult. The Golden Rule and the Decalogue were the essential ethical standards requisite for this development of school-children. Since there was "a broad, common ground, where all Christians and lovers of virtues meet," teachers were urged "to train up the rising generation in those elevated moral principles of the Bible" which did not impinge upon sectarian differences (Lewis, 1838, p. 7). Bushnell defended the Scriptures as an integral part of the common school curriculum while denying the legitimacy of sectarian teaching. (Bushnell, 1840). The responsibility of the public school, therefore, was to inculcate moral and religious values that were compatible with the rights of others and with democratic principles of government. The importance that was attached to this task is emphasized by one writer:

> This moral instruction based upon Biblical injunctions was thought to be an effective insurance for the promotion of a strong and viable republicanism throughout the land. If votes were bought and sold, the school would teach honesty; if political corruption was rampant, the school would inculcate honor and integrity; if fraud and falsehood abounded, the school would emphasize truth and justice. This was the glorious opportunity American society presented to public education. It was to prepare the nation's children to become literate, republican and Christian adults and thus guarantee generations of patriotic and moral citizens. (Lannie, 1975, p. 118)

THE CATHOLIC PAROCHIAL SCHOOL SYSTEM

Not all Americans were pleased with the "nondenominational, Bible-centered, Christian education" in the public schools. Many thinking Catholics rejected nondenominational Christianity as a workable compromise and alternative to teaching sectarian doctrines because they felt it was inimical to their religious faith. One practical result was that the bishops made widespread efforts to establish separate diocesan schools. By 1884 the parochial school system had been legislated as an indispensable component of American Catholicism. "Every Catholic child in a Catholic school" became the dominant theme (Lannie, 1975, p. 128).

With a private, religious school system, the Catholic Church was now free and able to teach its faith as it saw fit. The school day began with pupils kneeling to say their prayers. Religious instruction was included every day, and school was dismissed with prayer. An important part of the educational process was to let "the influence of religion" permeate the classroom during the entire school day. Schoolroom walls included religious pictures and statuary and such signs as: "Listen attentively to the Catechism." The goal was for the total environment to stimulate religious attitudes so that pupils could "learn to keep God in their minds all the days of their lives" (Murray, 1876). This meant that teachers were selected with special reference to their moral and religious character, and the attempt was made to surround the pupils with an atmosphere of religion and piety that reinforced the work of formal religious instruction. Thus, the "permeation theory" insisted that religious value formation took place not only through the intellectual content of the curriculum and the catechism and the training of pupils in pious practices, but in "the sum of all the educative influences of the schoolroom" (Burns, 1908, pp. 26, 27).

LEGAL ASPECTS

It was inevitable that some individual American citizens would object to any sort of religious expression within the public school classroom, even to Bible-reading without comment or to the recital of nonsectarian prayers. America had always prided itself on being "one nation under

God," but in the mid-twentieth century some irate citizens complained that God had no place in the classroom, and took the public schools to court.

McCollum Case

The first important case brought to the Supreme Court was the so-called McCollum case (*Illinois* ex. rel. *McCollum* v. *Board of Education*, 1948). A determined atheistic mother challenged the right of the Board of Education in Champaign, Illinois, to offer religious instruction in the public school classrooms during school hours. In 1940, Protestant, Jewish, and Roman Catholic leaders had banded together and formed the Champaign Council on Religious Education. This council obtained permission of the school board, hired instructors in religion, and asked parents to give voluntary permission for their children to attend classes in religion in the school building. Elementary children attended 30 minutes weekly and junior high pupils 45 minutes. Protestant children stayed in their regular classrooms, Roman Catholic and Jewish children went to other parts of the building. Pupils not participating went elsewhere in the building. Even though participation was voluntary, there was considerable pressure to join, so that by the second semester of the fifth year Terry McCollum was the only child not participating. One can only feel sympathy for this boy.

In its findings, the Supreme Court upheld the contention of Mrs. McCollum that this practice was a violation of the First Amendment and declared that the public school system must not be used by churches to help them teach sectarian religion. This did not mean, however, that the schools could not give full emphasis to the place of religion in American culture. Justice Jackson wrote:

Perhaps such subjects as math, physics, or chemistry are or can be secularized. But it would not seem practical to teach either the practice or appreciation of the arts if we are to forbid exposure of youth to any religious influences. Music without sacred music, architecture minus the Cathedral, or painting without scriptural themes would be eccentric and incomplete. . . . Even such a science as biology raises the issue between evolution and creation. . . . Certainly a course in English literature that omitted the Bible . . . would be pretty barren. . . . The fact is that . . . nearly everything in our culture worth transmitting, everything which gives meaning to life, is saturated with religious influences. . . . One can hardly respect a system of education that would leave the student wholly ignorant of the currents of religious thought that move the world society. (*Illinois* ex. rel. *McCollum* v. *Board of Education*, 1948)

The churches did have to take the teaching of sectarian religion out of the public school classroom, however. The schools adjusted by dismissing pupils to go to religious classes in other buildings near the school. Some school systems, like Fort Wayne, Indiana, dismissed pupils to mobile classrooms in trailers that had been purchased by the cooperating churches. Teachers were hired and trained by the churches. Some schools had to change the mechanics of registration, of reporting grades, and other things, to eliminate public school aid.

Brooklyn Case

But in 1952, the constitutionality of releasing pupils from public school classrooms to go to churches for religious instruction was contested in *Zorach* v. *Clauson*, or the Brooklyn case. In this case, the Supreme Court upheld the constitutionality of weekday released-time religious education. The majority opinion stated:

No one is forced to go to the religious education classroom, and no religious exercise of instruction is brought into the classrooms of the public schools. A student need not take religious instructions. He is left to his own desires as to the manner or time of his religious devotions, if any.

The Constitution does not say that in every and all respects there shall be a separation of Church and State. Rather it studiously defines the manner, the specific ways in which there shall be no concert or union or dependency one on the other. That is the common sense of the matter. Otherwise the state and religion would be aliens to each other —hostile, suspicious, and even unfriendly.

We find no constitutional requirement which makes it necessary for government to be hostile to religion and to throw its weight against efforts to widen the effective scope of religious instruction. The government may be neutral when it comes to competition between sects. It may not thrust any sect on any person. It may not make a religious observance compulsory, it may not coerce any one to attend church, to observe a religious holiday, or to take religious instruction. But it can close its doors to suspend its operations as to those who want to repair to their religious sanctuaries for worship or instruction. No more than that is undertaken here. (*Zorach* v. *Clauson,* 1952)

New York Regents Prayer Case

The third case was the New York Regents Prayer Case. As early as 1951, the New York State Board of Regents had composed a nonsectarian prayer to be recited in the classroom. The prayer was phrased in such a way as to be acceptable to Jews, Roman Catholics, and Protestants. The prayer read: "Almighty God, we acknowledge our dependence upon Thee, and we beg Thy blessings upon us, our parents, our teachers, and our country." The students were not compelled to recite the prayer, and, at parental request, they could be permitted to leave the classroom during the recital. However, the court felt that support by school authorities tended to be coercive. Rejection of this prayer by the Supreme Court in 1962 made it clear that the state should remain fully neutral on all religious questions (*Engel* v. *Vitale*, 1962).

Bible-Reading and Prayer

A fourth case was brought to the Supreme Court in 1963 by the parents of children in two states, Maryland and Pennsylvania, in protest of state requirements that made it obligatory to begin each day with prayer and Bible-reading without comment. The court ruled in favor of the parents and said that to require prayer and Bible-reading violated the principle of separation of church and state. This decision did allow the study of the Bible and religion when presented objectively as part of a secular program of education.

While the Supreme Court has declared in a series of decisions over the last two decades that prayer, religious observances, and sectarian teaching in public schools are unconstitutional, it has left untouched the schools' mandate to educate young people in the values and ideals of our society. These are often referred to as "democratic" values, but they are really "cultural" values that have a long standing both in our national history and in Western culture with its Judeo-Christian heritage (Hall, 1977, p. 277).

VALUES EDUCATION AND CLARIFICATION

Definition and Importance

A value is the relative worth, merit, or importance of something. When a person values something, he or she deems it worthwhile—worth having, worth doing, worth believing, or worth trying to obtain. A value may be a standard of conduct, of beauty, of efficiency, or of worth that people accept, maintain, or live up to. An aesthetic value refers to a standard of what is beautiful that people can enjoy. A moral value represents a standard of right and wrong. There are other types of values as well—monetary, for example (Fraenkel, 1977, pp. 6, 7).

Values are important because they tell us a great deal about the people who hold them. Different people value different things. Some people value things that are worth a great deal of money. Others place a greater value on human associations and relationships. The more we can find out about what people value, the better, for in so doing we learn a lot about what makes them tick—the kinds of decisions they are likely to make, the leaders they will follow, the politics they will endorse, and the things on which they are likely to spend their time, talents, and money. The study of values is a study of people—their priorities, goals, and preferences (Fraenkel, 1977, p. 10).

The Approach

One of the most widely used approaches to values education in the schools today is the values clarification approach espoused by Raths, Harmin, and Simon in their book *Values and Teaching* (1966). This approach attempts to get students to look more closely at their own ideas and behavior, so they can "clarify" for themselves what they really value. It does not aim to instill any particular set of values, or to moralize. Rather, the goal is to help students become more aware of their own feelings, ideas, choices, and behavior. Once they are aware of their values they can more consciously choose their priorities and move in the directions they want to go (Hall, 1973, p. 11).

The Process of Valuing

Raths and colleagues emphasize that true values must include seven important criteria, which may be divided into three processes, choosing, prizing, and acting, as follows:

Choosing: (1) freely
            (2) from alternatives
            (3) after thoughtful consideration of the consequences of each alternative
Prizing: (4) cherishing, being happy with the choice
            (5) willing to affirm the choice publicly
Acting: (6) doing something with the choice
            (7) repeatedly, in some pattern of life
                 (Raths, Harmin, and Simon, 1966, p. 30)

Thus, when persons value something, they choose it freely, without coercion, after careful consideration of all the alternatives—for without alternatives there would be no choice. Once they have made the choice, they are happy with it, glad they have made it, and willing to admit it publicly. This indicates that they still value it. Once chosen, the value is acted upon repeatedly, else it would not be of much value.

The above is a description of the *process* of valuing. Raths was interested in teaching students *how* to sort out values, not *what* to value. Students are encouraged to think their way through these seven steps, to become increasingly aware of the valuing process, to strengthen their own values and beliefs, and to align their behavior with them.

Strategies

A number of different authors have developed numerous exercises and strategies that may be used in the classroom to facilitate the process of values clarification. Here are only a few of the strategies that have been used:

Write down 20 things you like to do, and indicate beside each the cost (in dollars and cents) of doing it, whether you like to do it alone or with other people, whether or not planning is required, and when you did it last. Then from the 20 items, list the five most important. Discuss this with the class.

Values voting. The teacher presents a voting list to the students and prefaces it with: "How many of you . . ."

   . . . think there are times when cheating is justified?
   . . . watch TV more than three hours daily?
   . . . enjoy going to church or temple?
   . . . approve of premarital sex?
      etc.

This may be followed by class discussion.

Rank order. Students are asked to rank various items in order of preference, for example:

Where would you rather be on a Saturday afternoon?
   _____at the beach
   _____in the woods
   _____in a discount store

Which is most important in friendship?
   _____loyalty
   _____generosity
   _____honesty

Which would you give the lowest priority to today?
   _____space
   _____poverty
   _____defense
   _____ecology

Either-or forced choice. The teacher asks: Are you
   . . . more of a saver or a spender?
   . . . more of a loner or a grouper?
   . . . more physical or mental?
      etc.

Values continuum. Students are asked to arrange themselves in the proper position along a whole line of students to indicate their value position along the continuum. They might be asked, for example:

How far would you go to be popular with your group?

Do anything,	Do nothing
including risking	at
safety	all

Values whips. The teacher poses a question to the class, provides a few minutes for the students to decide on their answer, then whips around the class calling upon individuals to give their answers. Here are some sample questions:

What is something you really believe in strongly?

What is something you have done you are really proud of?

There are numerous other strategies that have been used:

Public interviews of individual students or of groups of students. The students are interviewed in front of the class.

Keeping a values journal whereby the students jot down their values as related to their feelings and actions.

Value sharing with a partner or two

Writing autobiographies that reveal values

(Simon et al., 1972)

Five Dimensions

In his book on *Advanced Value Clarification,* Kirschenbaum (1977) describes the value clarification process in terms of five important dimensions rather than in terms of seven as outlined by Raths. According to Kirschenbaum, value clarification is:

Thinking—about value decisions

Feeling— becoming aware of one's feelings so as to enable one to achieve goals more readily

Choosing—considering alternatives and doing achieve ment planning

Communicating—listening and talking with others and resolving conflicts, which helps in establishing goals and values

Acting—repeatedly, consistently, and skillfully in achieving one's goals

(Kirschenbaum, 1977)

Critique

Values clarification has not been without its critics. For example, can anyone really be objective about what he or she values? Psychologists would say it is most difficult. Does the fact of clarifying one's values improve morality? What if the values held are unworthy or superficial? Will values clarification get at the origin of these values and change them, if such is desired? What are the real objectives of the program, and to what extent may these be reached? One writer suggests that sharing one's personal values with others may bring a person into open conflict and create all sorts of problems. For example, if a pupil reveals values different from adults, he or she may run the risk of head-on collisions with teachers, parents, or employers.

In spite of some weaknesses, the values clarification approach to moral education is being widely used and with some success in stimulating thinking. Students are reported to be less apathetic, less conforming, and more energetic and critical in their thinking (Simon et al., 1972, p. 20).

EDUCATION FOR MORAL DECISION-MAKING

Goals

Another approach to moral education in the schools emphasizes making moral judgments on the highest possible level. This approach is based upon Kohlberg's three levels of moral development: the premoral level, the morality of convention, and the level of universally applicable principles. (See Chapter 3.) The attempt is to stimulate students to think about moral issues and to grow in their ability to make rational moral decisions at the highest levels. The goal is to develop students' moral reasoning with the expectation that this will improve moral behavior (Kirschenbaum, 1977, p. 43).

The Morally Educated Person

Wilson (1970, 1972) has suggested several characteristics of morally educated people.

First, they consider the feelings, needs, and interests of other people to be as important as their own. Without this attitude one would not even *need* to think morally, for one could feel perfectly free to use other people as one wished.

Second, morally educated people have insight into the needs, feelings, and interests of others. They know just what hurts people, what they need, and what is in their best interests.

Third, they have sufficient factual knowledge to be able with reasonable success to predict the outcome of their actions. One way to gain such knowledge is by having the ability to communicate fluently with a wide range of people.

Fourth, they have the desire to take the above three characteristics into account in making decisions. It is possible to know and understand but still make decisions on the basis of "what the majority of people do" or "what my parents say."

Fifth, they are alert and sensitive to situations where sound moral judgments are required.

Sixth, they apply to themselves the judgments they apply to others. In other words, they strive to *do* what they think is right (Wilson, 1970).

Principles of This Type of Moral Education

Several important principles are utilized in this type of moral education.

1. All discussion must take place in an atmosphere of openness and personal integrity. This demands teachers who are not afraid of various points of view, who are willing to be honest and open, and who do not try to indoctrinate students with their own ideas. One goal is to stimulate thought, not to squelch it. This means that a wide variety of solutions may be tolerated. The crucial question is not what is *the* solution, but what is a good solution, or what are good solutions? (Sullivan, 1975, p. 107).

2. The goal is not to teach facts or rules or particular value systems, but to teach the process by which moral decisions are made. This is not a program of indoctrination, but a program of education, which means it assists students in becoming more nearly autonomous, capable of making informed decisions of their own.

3. The method utilizes concrete experiences to which pupils can relate and which give them practice in moral reasoning and decision-making.

4. Pupils are taught to make judgments rationally by taking into account how those decisions affect the interests, feelings, needs, and lives of others. Thus, actions are judged to be right, wrong, good, or bad depending on their effects on others (Harris, 1976, p. 32).

Method

The primary method used in this type of teaching is to present case studies, or moral dilemmas for the students to solve. Here is one dilemma that is used to promote thinking and discussion.

Joe is a 14-year-old boy who wanted to go to camp very much. His father promised him he could go if he saved up the money for it himself. So Joe worked hard at his paper route and saved up the $40 it cost to go to camp and a little more besides. But just before camp was going to start, his father changed his mind. Some of his friends decided to go on a special fishing trip, and Joe's father was short of the money it would cost. So he told Joe to give him the money he had saved from the paper route. Joe didn't want to give up going to camp, so he thought of refusing to give his father the money. (Pagliuso, 1976, p. 126)

The students are then presented with a number of questions:

Should Joe refuse to give his father the money? Why? Why not?

What do you think of the father asking Joe for the money?

Does giving the money have anything to do with being a good son?

Should promises always be kept?

The students might also be asked to respond to the following:

Joe wanted to go to camp but he was afraid to refuse to give his father the money. So he gave his father $10 and told him that was all he made. He took the other $40 and paid for camp with it. He told his father the head of the camp said he could pay later. So he went off to camp, and the father didn't go on the fishing trip. Before Joe went to camp, he told his older brother, Alexander, that he really made $50 and that he lied to his father and said he'd made $10. Alexander wonders whether he should tell his father or not. (Pagliuso, 1976, p. 128)

This dilemma raises a number of important issues: whether lying is ever justified; whether withholding the truth is justified, or tattling is justified; whether it is more important for Alex to be a loyal son or a loyal brother.

Should Joe have lied?
Should Alex tell his father?
What should the father do if he finds out?

Teachers need to make up incidents that relate to the students' own lives, which are meaningful to them. But they might also raise questions regarding moral issues and social concerns (Hall and Davis, 1975). In using moral social issues, teachers are urged to use cases that are scaled to the level and interests of those being asked to make the decision. Otherwise the student will not be affected because he or she will have little interest in what is being discussed. Thus the student may be keenly interested in whether or not to get an abortion, and under what circumstances, but be quite uninterested in whether or not abolitionists should have helped slaves escape before the Civil War.

Results

The real question, after all, is: Does moral education work? Limited research tends to indicate that students learn to reason at a slightly higher moral level after extensive discussion of moral issues (Mantz, 1978, p. 16). But this is only part of the question. Assuming that students develop improved judgmental capacities, will this actually produce more mature conduct in conflict situations? Kohlberg himself maintains that "in addition to stimulating the development of general moral judgment capacities, a developmental moral education would stimulate the child's application of his own moral judgments (not the teacher's) to his actions" (Kohlberg, 1966, p. 28). At the present time, however, there is not sufficient evidence to show that, because students think in deeper moral terms, they thereby conduct themselves more morally. Mantz suggests:

For schools to credit moral education with reducing vandalism or drug abuse or teen-age pregnancies would be as extravagant as if the schools were blamed for all these evils. (Mantz, 1978, p. 24)

In spite of the uncertainties, the trend toward both moral education and values clarification is growing. Many educators argue that the schools can no longer dodge moral issues, and this is an educator's way of dealing with them.

12
The Churches
and Religious Education

THE POSITIVE INFLUENCE OF THE CHURCH

To what extent is the church having an influence on the morals of today's youths? This is a hard question to answer since there are youths whom the church has never touched, as well as many others who have been influenced to a considerable extent. The fact is that the churches have changed the lives of countless thousands of young people. Recently, the pastor of a local Congregational church returned with his youth group from a week-long windjammer cruise along the Maine coast. During the week, two young men deepened their Christian commitment and decided to become ministers of the church. This is evidence of the positive influence of the church in action.

Declining Influence
There is a feeling, however, among both adults and young people that the influence of the church is waning. The church is accused of being too materialistic, of lacking dynamic leadership, of abandoning traditional standards of Christian ethics, of showing a general lack of spiritual values (Eppel and Eppel, 1966, p. 52). A thirty-seven-year study of freshmen at Harvard and Clark universities

showed that attitudes toward the church declined considerably over the thirty-seven years prior to 1970 (Jones, 1970). For example, 78 percent of the early group and 17 percent of the later group agreed with the statement: "I think the church is a divine institution and it commands the highest loyalty and respect." This increased disaffection with the church, however, was only partially accompanied by a less favorable attitude toward religion in general. The proportion who said that religion had little or no influence on their ethical conduct only increased from 25 to 30 percent. The students were disillusioned with the established church's teachings and practices in relation to current social, civic, and economic problems, but at the same time many expressed a marked interest in a variety of religions and religious experiences (Jones, 1970).

Religious Concerns

The fact remains that many youths still express deep religious concerns. One of the most widely used instruments for surveying these concerns has been the Mooney Problem Check List. The Check List identifies eleven problem areas, each with thirty specific problems, making it possible to arrange clusters of problems as well as specific difficulties. This Check List was administered to 583 male and female freshmen and sophomores at Michigan State University (Bert-Hallahmi, 1974). Seventeen out of thirty items on the Morals and Religion scale covered religious concerns and conflicts. The percentage of students checking each of these concerns is given in Table 12-1. As can be seen, five out of seventeen concerns were checked by at least 25 percent of the students. Four of these concerns deal with the belief crises that students are going through. The fifth relates to the decline in church attendance. All reflect confusion and change involved in the "loss of faith" (Bert-Hallahmi, 1974, p. 337).

The reader must be cautioned to remember that any measurement of adolescent concern over religion depends a lot on what is included under religion: specific beliefs, dogma, philosophy of life, values, personal ethics, morals, or behavior. Adolescents are concerned about their personal morality; they are concerned about a philosophy of life. Thus, they are interested in religion (Rice, 1978, p. 497).

Religiosity and Social Deviancy

The fact remains, however, that religious involvement is the single most important factor in predicting the social behavior of adolescents. In general, those who are church members, who attend church, and who are involved in church activities are least likely to be involved in delinquent activities, in using illicit drugs, in using alcohol and marijuana, and in premarital sexual activity (Albrecht et al., 1977, pp. 263, 264). A recent study of 244 Mormon teenagers in three western states showed a high correlation, especially for boys, between participation in religious activities and absence of social deviancy (Albrecht et al., 1977).

PROBLEMS IN RELIGIOUS EDUCATION

If the churches are to meet the religious needs of even the majority of youths in this country, some very real problems will have to be overcome.

Time Factors

One problem has to do with time—with the amount of time youths are exposed to church influences versus the amount of time they are under other influences. I have

Table 12-1
Percentage of students (N—583)
checking each of the religion items
on the Mooney Problem Check List

Item No. on Check List	Item Content	Percentage
204	Confused in some of my religious beliefs	29.8
36	Not going to church often enough	29.5
40	Doubting the value of worship and prayer	26.4
93	Don't know what to believe about God	26.4
203	Wanting to feel close to God	25.1
39	Losing my earlier religious faith	24.0
37	Dissatisfied with church services	22.7
38	Having beliefs that differ from my church	19.0
202	Wanting to understand more about the Bible	14.7
91	Differing from my family in religious beliefs	8.7
149	Affected by racial or religious prejudice	8.5
147	Missing spiritual elements in college life	8.3
148	Troubled by lack of religion in others	8.2
94	Science conflicting with my religion	7.7
150	In love with somebody of a different race or religion	7.2
92	Failing to see the relation of religion to life	7.0
201	Wanting more chances for religious worship	6.2

Adapted from B. Bert-Hallahmi, "Self-reported Religious Concerns of University Underclassmen," *Adolescence* 9 (1974) :335. Used by permission.

already mentioned in Chapter 10 that by the time of graduation from high school the average child has spent 20,000 hours watching television, and 11,000 hours in the school classroom, but only 400 hours in religious education, assuming a religious attendance of one hour every other week for sixteen years. Considering the amount of exposure children get from the church, it is remarkable that the church is able to exert any influence at all. If the public schools had only a comparable amount of time, our children would be illiterate. Obviously, children are exposed to religious influences outside the church building, particularly in the family. Otherwise they would be religious illiterates. One task of the churches is to find ways to increase the hours children and youths spend under their influence. Specific suggestions will be given later in this chapter.

Competition with Other Activities

The churches are also competing with many other organizations for the time of their young people. Let us assume high school students are in school until 2:30 in the afternoon, are working after school or enrolled in sports and other extracurricular activities, and are doing homework on school nights. They go out Friday and Saturday nights, sleep late Saturday morning, and sometimes on Sunday. When do they have time for church activities? Traditionally, Sunday is for church, but the churches are hard pressed to keep that time for themselves. Many youths work part-time on that day. I've always been annoyed at all the extracurricular school activities that seem to continually press in on the little amount of time available on Sundays. Many times my young people told me they couldn't come to Fellowship because of a meeting at school, a play rehearsal, and so on.

Christian stewardship demands that we put first things first and learn to budget our time to give sufficient attention to things of the Spirit. But when so many adult community leaders and groups demand so much time of our young people, it's hard for them to resist. Pastors and other church leaders can discuss the problem with other youth-serving agencies and try to work out suitable arrangements. And they should not hesitate to try to get young people themselves to include a time commitment as part of their total commitment to Christ and his church.

Lack of Parental Cooperation

The church functions best when it gets the total cooperation of the parents. The churches found out years ago that they can't do the whole job themselves; they can only supplement parental influences. The major responsibility for Christian nurture still remains within the family. This is the meaning of Baptism, and this is the philosophy reflected in several church school curricula that supply home reading books to be used in the family. However, the churches have difficulty getting parents to attend special meetings where these things can be explained and instructions given. Many parents take baptismal vows to bring up their children "in the nurture and admonition of the Lord" and then do very little in a formal way to keep those vows. The churches may have to put the responsibility for Christian nurture squarely in the hands of the parents and let them know that this is exactly what Baptism means.

One of the things I will always remember about my upbringing was mother reading Bible stories to us before bedtime. Not only did we enjoy the stories, but it was a warm, intimate time for family members to be together, and the good it accomplished went far beyond the Biblical knowledge gained. The same was true of family devotions. *Today* magazine (now called *These Days*), plus the Bible, graced the breakfast table. These were regularly read by us before school. Grace at the table, dutifully offered by our father, was also a positive influence.

No Contact

Today there are large numbers of youths with whom the churches have no contact, because they never enter the churches' doors. The churches try everything: youth recreational centers, basketball leagues, youth evangelism, youth clubs and organizations of various kinds. By and large, these activities reach middle-class young people who are already busily involved in many other endeavors. There are still the large groups of nonjoiners, the street youngsters, who are not reached by any formal, middle-class youth activity. Some pastors and youth workers take to the streets; others establish coffee houses, halfway houses, drug rehabilitation centers, and other special ministries. No one group or activity reaches all young people, but the total number of youths the churches serve goes far beyond the number attending Sunday school, worship, and youth fellowship. The total of activities offered is staggering, and is limited only by the resources that adult church members are willing to commit to a variety of youth ministries.

Lack of Commitment

While the churches ask young people to pledge their faith and loyalty to Jesus Christ at the time they join the church, this is sometimes not spelled out in specific enough terms for youths to apply to their lives. We are far too bashful about asking youths to make definite commitments that are concrete expressions of their faith in Christ.

We need to insist that joining the church means active support through attendance, service, gifts, and prayers. But what does this mean? More specific suggestions need to be spelled out. Why not ask for pledges—on a series of short-term bases—for participation in youth study groups, for several hours a week in working for the church, or for service during the summer months in a mission project? Youths need to be challenged. They want to feel they are doing something, that they are making sacrifices. We have been far too bashful about asking young people to give of themselves.

The Temptation to Be Secular

One problem I always had as a minister of Christian education was in keeping youth activities relevant to the purpose of the church. Of course, anything that helps youth grow into well-rounded, mature adults is a legitimate activity. Youth want to have dances, hayrides, picnics, and outings. They need numerous and varied social activities. They want to have fun through the church—and they should. Churches should not hesitate to minister to these needs of their youths. But youth leaders need to be vigilant to ensure that youth activities also include study, worship, discussion, instruction, and service. I am particularly fond of small-group discussions in which the religious concerns of youths are expressed. The churches have to be certain that youth activities are designed to foster spiritual growth and nurture as well as social growth. If the churches don't fulfill their unique spiritual functions, who else will?

Irrelevant

I am also convinced that part of what the churches do is irrelevant to the lives of the youths they serve. There are many important theological and ethical questions which young people are asking that need to be dealt with. One of the church's most important tasks is to deal with these immediate questions. How about a youth fellowship group or Sunday school class based entirely on present religious concerns and questions of young people? The Bible and other reading materials can be used in searching for answers. But there is a need to start where youth are in helping them to grow in their understanding.

APPROACHES

What are some of the ways the churches can overcome these difficulties in meeting the religious needs of youths, and in having an influence on their morals?

Begin Early

One way is by beginning early in the child's life—before the child begins attending public school kindergarten. This means offering a weekday church nursery school in addition to the usual Sunday nursery school class. A firm foundation of Christian nurture can be laid with children from three to five years of age—provided the school offers a real program of Christian education, and not just the nursery school experiences that one would find in a secular day-care center. Specifically I mean story material, creative activities, music, prayers, and worship geared to these age levels, but Christian in content and purpose—in keeping with the total program of Christian education in the church. There is a temptation to be completely secular so that the church nursery is no different from the community nursery downtown. There *should* be a difference.

Weekday Religious Education

If we are going to accomplish the task, we need more than an hour or so on Sunday morning. This means sponsoring weekday religious education classes for school-age children, kindergarten through grade 8. I am much in favor of released-time classes, where pupils are dismissed from public school for one period, one day a week, to go to religious classes in their own churches or in other places. Attendance is far more regular than at Sunday school, teachers are better trained (they are often professionals, and sometimes paid as well), and activities and curricula are carefully chosen and planned. Parents and church leaders should put their influence behind the establishment of weekday religious education classes in their communities if such do not exist. These are best done cooperatively with other churches.

Vacation Church School

Vacation church school for kindergarten through eighth grade provides a valuable opportunity for religious instruction. Because classes meet five days a week, usually two and a half hours daily, for two weeks, there are opportunities for projects and activities that require longer periods of time than are available during regular Sunday church school hours. Pupils receive about twenty-five hours of religious instruction: this is as much as many receive during the whole Sunday school year if they attend half the time. Daily instruction allows for more continuity to the program, and I feel that more learning takes place. Usually the best, most committed teachers are willing to give of themselves during the summer months.

Summer Camps and Conferences

I believe these are the very best opportunities to reach young people with an intensive, inspiring, enlightening, and well-rounded program of Christian education. Camps are usually conducted for juniors, junior highs, and senior highs. I feel that senior high youths especially benefit from such a program. They are at the perfect age to profit most from the informal inquiry and discussion that takes place in such programs. Thousands of youths have made personal commitments to Christ as a result of the influence of summer church conferences and camps.

Family camps, which are under church sponsorship, are also good opportunities for the whole family to study, play, and worship together. Parents can receive valuable help in learning important principles of child development, and especially in understanding the Christian nurture of children and youth. Special times are set aside for family devotions, which can establish beneficial habits that can be continued back home.

Retreats

Weekend or holiday retreats during the school year also allow far greater exposure than is possible through regular church school and youth fellowship programs. Retreats are also a way of reaching teenagers who do not attend other activities or services. Youths find such experiences a lot of fun, helpful, and inspirational. Youths who tend to be shy and socially awkward in other situations find the informal retreat experience a good way of making close friends as well as an instrument for Christian growth.

Spiritual Research Groups

These may be called prayer cells or Bible study groups, but I like the term "spiritual research groups." Such an especially constituted group can meet over a specified period of time for informal discussion, and for prayer if desired. Some churches establish such groups during Lent, for example. Groups can meet anytime, but many prefer times when youths don't ordinarily get together: before school, for breakfast, for lunch, or right after school. Weekly meetings assure continuity. The group should be informal—allowing for maximum opportunity for discussion. The discussion may be based on something the group reads out loud together or on specific religious questions or problems that individual members bring up, or it may be centered around specific moral dilemmas. The "moral dilemmas" approach that the schools use can be profitably employed in these groups. (See Chapter 11.)

Individual Reading

Churches need to urge young people to read more good religious literature—especially during the summer months when more leisure time is available. Some churches keep a fine library of books appropriate for young people. Biographical stories of missionaries and other church heroes are especially appealing to youths and help them to gain a solid understanding of church history and of the missionary activities of the church. Some churches even give special recognition to youths for the reading they have done. This acts as a stimulus and helps publicize opportunities for other youths to do likewise.

Sunday Church School

I have never had much success with Sunday school for high school adolescents. Only a small percentage attend. A significant number prefer to go to church, since they consider Sunday school "kid stuff" and much beneath their dignity. Junior highs present problems in discipline. The small numbers of senior highs who attend are the old faithfuls who go to everything. I believe we should continue Sunday school for all ages, but I've never been able to attract a majority of youths who are members of the church. This is really a shame, because just when they are old enough to absorb solid Christian teaching, they quit coming. I've always liked the kinds of materials the denominations put out for Sunday school for teenagers. Yet youths miss out. Perhaps we should find alternative times to use these materials, and find more creative ways of promoting church and youth fellowship. There is no rule which says that church school classes have to be only on Sunday morning.

Youth Church

Some congregations offer a worship service especially for young people, with the sermon addressed to them and reflecting their concerns, and with the youths themselves helping to lead the service.

Summer Service

Enlisting youths in national and local mission service projects during the summer is an extremely valuable way of helping adolescents to become acquainted with the wider work of the church and in helping them to expand their horizons and concerns and to deepen their commitment to Christ and his church.

Youth Fellowship

Several of the major Protestant groups have given up their traditional fellowship organizations after finding it increasingly difficult to interest their young people in them. Some of the "canned programs" have been fairly dull and irrelevant, or the organizational structure has gotten in the way. The trend seems to be toward having less formal, less structured group activities based upon needs of members, rather than following closely the structures and programs set down by national headquarters.

Youth Choir

The youth choir presents a unique opportunity for young people to become acquainted with sacred music, participate regularly in the worship of the church, and do something together on a planned basis to serve their church. The youth choir promotes good fellowship, Christian learning, reverence and worship, and Christian stewardship. It is another way of reaching youths whom the church might not interest in other ways.

Parental Instruction

Any church that does not also instruct parents in the why, the what, and the how of Christian nurture is not doing a complete job. Most parents want to raise their teenagers as good Christians, but many need help because they don't know how, or, if they do, aren't doing it. This is the church's task—to put the responsibility squarely on their shoulders and then to give guidance and direction in accomplishing the task. It is my hope, for example, that this book can be used with groups of parents who seek fuller understanding of the moral development of youths. Why not have parent classes on the subject?

OUR GOAL

The goal of Christian education is well stated in a study paper called *The Objective of Christian Education for Senior High Young People*. It states:

> The objective of Christian education is to help persons to be aware of God's self-disclosure and seeking love in Jesus Christ, and to respond in faith and love—to the end that they may know who they are and what their human situation means, grow as sons of God rooted in the Christian community, live in the Spirit of God in every relationship, fulfill their common discipleship in the world, and abide in the Christian hope. (Cully, 1963, p. 171)

Part IV
MORAL BEHAVIOR

13
God's Plan
and Vocational Choice

GOD'S PLAN FOR EVERY HUMAN LIFE

One of the tasks that Christian parents and youth leaders share is to help young people discover meaning in life. Unless there is a purpose for living, why live at all? Why spend some threescore years and ten on this earth without knowing why? It is as senseless to live without a purpose for living as it is to go to college without a reason for going. Life must have meaning or purpose, else we only feel useless and unnecessary.

Christianity has a great deal to say about the meaning of existence. And at the heart of all Christian teaching is this important truth: God has a definite purpose for every human life, a life plan for every person, and one's purpose in living can only be accomplished if that person seeks to discover God's plan for his or her life and to follow it.

This means that God has something to say about where people work and what type of work they perform. He has something to say about whom they marry and what kind of home life they are to have. He has something to say about their relationships to their friends. God has a plan which young people need to discover and which requires commitment before they can live it.

There are at least two reasons why we know God has a plan for each person's life. The first reason is related to the planning that is so evident in the physical world around us. One often hears the remark: "I can't plan on anything these days. The world is so upset. Everything is topsy-turvy. I never know what to expect next."

Such a remark might describe our human relationships, but it cannot accurately describe the physical world in which we live. Very few of us were concerned about whether the sun would rise this morning. We knew it would. We have little doubt that spring will come as it always has. The new spring styles are designed months ahead of time. The advertising layouts are completed before Christmas—in anticipation of the sure coming of spring. Nor are we afraid that the law of gravity will change and we will find ourselves floating against the ceiling. When a jet pilot takes off in his new plane, he doesn't worry about whether the laws of aerodynamics will change. He knows they do not change. His only concern is that his plane has been built so as to make the best use of the laws of nature so that he can have a safe and speedy journey home. The weatherman who seeks to predict to-morrow's sunshine or rain knows that the laws governing the weather do not change, else he could not use those laws in making predictions. The research chemist who combines two elements in the same proportions and under the same chemical conditions knows each time that the product will be the same. Because of this planning in the world in which we live, astronomers are able to predict years ahead when the next eclipse of the sun will be, and at what moments the tides will rise and fall. The hunter who arises early on a winter morning does so with the hope that this is the day the ducks are moving to the warmer waters of the south.

Yes, everywhere the wonders of nature reveal order and planning in the universe. And if God has a plan for the physical universe, it is logical to assume that he has a plan for his highest creation—for people. We discover, by observing our physical world, that God operates according to a purpose, that he is a planning Creator. God's world is in order; it is only the little world that man has tried to create for himself that is confusion and chaos.

The second reason why we believe that God has a plan for each life is because of the life of Christ. Here too we see planning and purpose. Jesus said: "For I have come down from heaven, not to do my own will, but the will of him who sent me" (John 6:38). Throughout his ministry, Jesus worked under the assumption that God had a plan for his life, and that his own task was to accomplish the purposes of God. He lived with this realization of God's purposes during all of his earthly life. While agonizing in prayer in the Garden of Gethsemane Jesus committed himself completely to God's plan. "Father, if thou art willing, remove this cup from me; nevertheless not my will, but thine, be done" (Luke 22:42).

No one of us would dare to think that the life or death of Christ was without plan or purpose. Everything Jesus did revealed the wise counsel of God. And Jesus lived and died to show that just as God had a plan for his life, so also he has one for ours. Christ's task was primarily one of revelation, of unveiling the mind of God to the world. In so doing, he revealed that God has a plan and a purpose for us.

THE CHRISTIAN CONCEPT OF VOCATION

The next important principle that Christian parents and youth leaders ought to try to develop is the concept of Christian vocation.

First, what is meant when we speak of a Christian vocation? If we examine the words individually, we discover some interesting ideas. The word "Christian" was first applied in the first century A.D. to those apostles in Antioch who acknowledged Christ as Lord. Thus, they were called Christian or "those of Christ." The word "vocation," like the word "vocal," comes from the Latin *vocare,* meaning "to call." A vocation then is a call or summons. And a Christian vocation is a call to Christlikeness. To follow a Christian vocation implies living according to the principles of Jesus, particularly in one's chosen field of work. It involves acknowledging Christ as Lord of one's life.

The term "Christian vocation" was never intended to apply only to church vocations. A person does not have to be a minister, a Christian educator, a missionary, a church secretary, or a social worker to have a Christian career. For whether or not a particular occupation is a Christian one depends upon the person—upon whether the individual considers his or her lifework just a job, or a real calling. If it is just a job, the person does it halfheartedly and often grudgingly, or only for personal profit or gain, without regard for fellow human beings, and without trying to serve Christ or to glorify him in what is done. If, however, one's work expresses one's calling, the person strives to do it as a service to God and to his kingdom. In other words, it is not only the kind of work that counts, but how it is done, and for what reason. The most menial task can be a Christian calling under the

Lordship of Christ

This means that if a person goes into science, then science should become an exciting adventure, a quest to understand and to know the laws of God in nature. And once these laws are understood they can be used for the benefit of everyone, not for personal or group power, and not to destroy, but to build. Whether science is a Christian career or not depends on the scientist, not on the profession. Those physicists, chemists, and engineers who objected to using knowledge of the atom in the creation of an atomic bomb were perfectly justified in questioning the use to which scientific knowledge was to be put. Science is supposed to be concerned only with the physical world, but scientists who are Christian must concern themselves with ethical principles and human relationships as well.

I shall never forget walking through the scattered, atomized bits of rubble of the city of Hiroshima, Japan. It was in the fall of 1945, only a few weeks after the bomb had been dropped, the bomb that killed 100,000 people and maimed twice that number in an instant. I had seen cities destroyed by war before, but never one that had been blown into so many small pieces. Small, grotesque globs of melted glass, a few broken and blackened tree stumps and telephone poles, and an occasional reinforced concrete building, largely shattered and completely gutted on the inside by fire—these were all that remained of the once proud city of Hiroshima.

No, it is not enough to be just a scientist. One must be a scientist and a Christian, or a politician and a Christian, or a statesman and a Christian, if one's efforts are to glorify God and benefit others. This means that if a Christian goes into business, he or she needs to be a Christian business person. One man that I know resigned as an executive of a large corporation because he objected to the shady practices of the executive board. The man wanted to make the business succeed, yes. He had twenty-five years of his life wrapped up in that company, but he did not want success more than he wanted fair play and ethical dealings with other companies and with his own employees. Since the man could not change the minds of his fellow executives, he changed jobs, finding employment where he could be both a businessman and a Christian.

This principle means that if someone goes into teaching, that person has a chance as a Christian to mold the minds and lives of tomorrow's leaders, a chance to make the classroom a school for Christ. Or the teacher can see the job only as an opportunity to work from 8 until 4 and a way to bring home a paycheck which is never adequate and which alone can never be satisfying.

This principle means that if someone goes into health care—for example as a physician, dentist, or nurse—that the person has a chance to minister to the bodies and souls of men, women, and children who are in pain, anxious, and sorrowing. Each patient can be treated as a child of God who is of infinite worth, or each patient can be considered another account number, another person who interrupts sleep and who is often unfair in what is demanded. There is a world of difference between a nurse—and a nurse who is a Christian.

What I am suggesting is that whether a job becomes a Christian vocation or not depends on the person: how the person does it and for what reason.

With these thoughts in mind, let us go on to discover the process by which Christian young people can choose a vocation. Once they discover that God has a plan for them, and that God wants whatever vocation they choose to be

Christian, they need additional guidance in the procedure for choosing. The following ideas are ones that I have used with young people and have found effective. I will present these ideas as though I were addressing them to teenagers themselves.

THE PROCESS OF CHOOSING A VOCATION

The first step in choosing a vocation is to surrender and commit your whole life to God. This is necessary in order that God may reveal his will to you. The important thing to remember is that God is right now trying to establish communications with you. He is calling you to be his own. He is like a friend who has picked up a telephone to call your number. Your phone is ringing and you have only to choose to pick up your receiver to answer God's call.

But before you receive God's word a basic decision has to be made. You have to decide whether or not you want to surrender the privacy of your life. Once you have a telephone installed you have given up your privacy, because you have agreed, at least by implication, to answer when your phone rings. If you refuse to answer and refuse often enough, your friends will stop calling and your telephone will be useless.

God works in a similar fashion. To receive him you surrender your privacy, that is, the right to run your own life. When you do, your telephone is installed. To learn of God's plan for your life you must completely surrender yourself to him, and say: "O.K., God, here I am, you tell me what to do." There can be no reservations when you make your commitment. When you answer you do not know beforehand what God is going to say. Your telephone may carry unhappy news. You may have to listen to something you would rather not hear. But you must answer when the phone rings or else the calls will stop coming.

Discovering God's plan is not so much a matter of knowledge as it is a matter of willing. Obedience, not mind, is the organ of spiritual knowledge. If you are willing, then you will know. Say to God: "I want to know and to follow completely your plan. You take over my life and tell me what you want me to do."

After this basic decision is made, the second step is to try to discover what you feel is the greatest need in your life and in the world. Do you feel your greatest need is to get married and to raise children? Do you desire to work for better housing or better standards of living, or to strengthen the churches of the community? Do you feel the greatest need is for better schools, improved medical care? Would you rather work to help the aged find their rightful place in society? Perhaps you feel the greatest needs arise out of world problems? Do you want to work for better relations among races and nations, or to strengthen the hope for world peace, or to advance scientific knowledge? The particular need that challenges you the most may be God's way of telling you that his plan for you is to work to fulfill those needs.

But the third step in choosing a vocation is to try to ascertain whether or not there is really an opportunity to fulfill the need you discover. You may feel, for example, that the world's greatest need is for education. But as you survey the teaching profession you discover that the teachers colleges are already cutting down enrollments and that there are only a limited number of opportunities for employment once you graduate. In such cases, you might look at opportunities for teaching in other communities, other states, or other parts of the world. I know of rural areas in my own state of Maine, for example, that have difficulty in getting teachers while the larger cities have a surplus of applicants. Are there opportunities for employment and service in locations other than the ones where you have already looked? Or are there greater opportunities for employment in other completely different fields? Ideally, the wisest choice would be one in which you feel there is the most need and in which there are the greatest opportunities. School guidance personnel can usually tell you what opportunities might be available in fields in which you are interested.

The fourth step is to discover what training and talents are needed in the occupation you are considering. Before an intelligent decision can be made concerning a particular vocation, it is necessary to get all the facts. Exactly what does the work involve? What training is necessary? Can you find ways and means of obtaining the education needed? What particular talents and abilities are needed for the job? Do you have the scholastic aptitude required? Can you develop the skills required? One way of answering these questions is to get information from (1) successful persons who are working in the field, and (2) library books and pamphlets on the vocation. It is also helpful to discover your own abilities and aptitudes by taking a series of vocational interest and aptitude tests.

The fifth step is to keep searching until you find what it is that God is trying to tell you to do. One of the basic teachings of the Bible is that God reveals his will to individual persons; God calls individual people. But this call need not be a dramatic one, such as a flash of light from heaven, a bolt of thunder, a mysterious dream, or a mystical experience. You may find your calling in the ordinary events of life. As you take different subjects in school, you will like some and hate others. Some will be easy, some hard, but the more you study the more you will come to the conviction that this field is for you and that one is not. You may come to a conclusion while reading the morning headlines in the local newspaper, or while talking to a friend, or while enjoying a late date. (There have been many important decisions made on late dates.) One of the most important decisions of my own life came while studying a college catalog.

God speaks to us in the ordinary, common events of our lives. He guides us through other people, by opening some doors, some opportunities for us, and by closing others. He guides us through and in the pages of the Bible.

One principle to remember is that God will never tell you to do anything that is contrary to his word. One man was admitted to a mental hospital because he said that God told him to kill his mother-in-law, and he did. Obviously, this wasn't the voice of God, but of his own hatred, jealousy, or anger.

If you pray to God to guide and reveal himself to you, and then keep alert to recognize God speaking to you, you will find the answer. I can't say exactly how God will speak to you, but I know he will, if you look for his revelation to you.

Two final words of caution need to be mentioned. First: Don't be surprised if God leads you into something that you may have been avoiding for a long time. Many a minister started out in life as an engineer, or in business, or some other field. One that I know used to be a song and dance man in Hollywood.

The second word of caution is: Don't be in too big a hurry if you can't find the answer at once. Sometimes God's revelation comes as a slowly dawning awareness. At other times the answer doesn't come until we feel blocked and ready to give up. The children of Israel found their way blocked when they came to the Red Sea. The Egyptian chariots were rushing them from behind. It was only when the people came to the sea, and during the last hours, that the waters opened, and the way was found through which to pass.

14
Marriage and Family Values

In a recent nationwide survey of high school seniors, 17,-
000 young people were asked to rate the importance of a
list of major life goals (Bachman and Johnston, 1979, p. 79).
The goals included such things as a good marriage and
family life, strong friendships, finding purpose and meaning in my life, finding steady work, being successful in my
work, making a contribution to society, having lots of
money, and being a leader in my community. The students were asked to rank each of these goals as "Extremely
important," "Quite important," "Somewhat important,"
or "Not important." The one goal that students ranked as
more important than any other was "having a good marriage and family life" (Bachman and Johnston, 1979, p. 80).
Nearly four out of five respondents ranked this goal as
extremely important.

In an earlier survey, over 3,000 youths from across the
nation indicated that having love was their most important personal value (Yankelovich, 1974, p. 66). And in a
nationwide survey among women of all ages the Roper
Organization found that only 4 percent of these women
desired a career without marriage. While the majority (52
percent) wanted marriage, children, and a career, 38 percent would settle for marriage and children without a

career. Only 4 percent, however, wanted marriage and a career without children, and only 1 percent would accept marriage only (Roper Organization, 1974). The results of these surveys indicate that American young people place a very high priority on marriage, love, and having a family, and that, in spite of the increasing numbers of women pursuing careers through gainful employment, the majority still place marriage and having children highest on their list of priorities. A great number also want a career in addition to family life.

Along with this continuing interest in marriage and family living, youths also evidence increasing skepticism and caution about the chances of marriage succeeding. When I asked a college coed: "What do you think of when you think of marriage?" her reply was: "Divorce." This girl along with other youths are well aware of the rise in divorce rates. Many young people have suffered through the experience of their parents' divorce. Or, they all see how unhappy their friends have been, and how often these marriages break up, and they become quite skeptical and concerned and say: "I'm not going to get married until I'm thirty." Or: "I have my career to worry about first, then there will be time enough to think about marriage." At other times their concern manifests itself in a desire not to duplicate marital tragedy in their own lives. "When I get married it's going to be different," is a resolution typically heard. Or some, searching for better ways of choosing a life partner, conclude: "I wouldn't think of getting married without living with a person first" (Rice, 1979, p. 3).

The Christian religion has some important things to say about marriage and family living, and these things need to be heard by our young people. Christian parents and teachers, therefore, have a continuing responsibility to teach the highest ideals that they know. In so doing, they can better enable their children to find the loving fulfillment they seek. My purpose in this chapter is to summarize some of these ideas which I feel need to be emphasized.

MARRIAGE AS GOD'S PLAN

The traditional marriage service begins with the recognition that marriage has been established by God for the benefit of humankind. The following is typical of such a service:

> Dearly beloved, we are assembled here in the presence of God, to join this Man and this Woman in holy marriage; which is instituted of God, regulated by His commandments, blessed by our Lord Jesus Christ, and to be held in honor among all men. Let us therefore reverently remember that God has established and sanctified marriage, for the welfare and happiness of mankind. (*The Book of Common Worship,* 1946, p. 183)

Part of God's plan for people is that they should not live alone. "It is not good that the man should be alone; I will make him a helper fit for him" (Gen. 2:18). Achtemeier suggests that a more exact meaning of the Hebrew text is "a helper corresponding to him" (Achtemeier, 1976, p. 12). This "corresponding" helper is one who matches body to body, mind to mind, spirit to spirit, hunger to hunger, who cares in response to being cared for, who loves and is loved. This is the person with whom one can share one's whole life. Marriage becomes the antidote for loneliness, the means by which the needs for love and companionship are met at the deepest possible level. Admittedly, this is a high ideal, and not always achieved in the marital relationship, but we are talking here about marriage as God intended it to be, so that we can present a goal toward which all can strive. The world as created by God was intended to be "very good" (Gen. 1:31) and marriage shares in that basic nature of "goodness" (Achtemeier, 1976, p. 16).

At the same time, however, the Bible recognizes that marriage may not be for everybody, so that no one should feel pressured into getting married because family and friends expect it or because it is "the thing to do." Both Jesus and the apostle Paul taught by word and example that some persons may feel called to remain single for the sake of doing God's work and will (Matt. 19:10–12; I Cor. 7:7). Some of the problems of marriage develop because youths get married for the wrong reasons: because of pregnancy, as means of escaping from an unhappy home or an unsatisfying personal life, or as a means of hurting or getting back at parents or an ex-lover. Other people get married because "everyone is doing it" and they don't want to be left "out of the swim." One high school girl told me that after graduation she was getting married because "there is nothing else to do." In a society that overromanticizes marriage and overcriticizes staying single, it's hard to resist the temptation to get married simply as a means of avoiding condemnation. Friends and family continually pressure the single man or woman: "When are you going to get married?" "Why don't you settle down?" Marriage is held up as the most desirable state of being, and those who remain single are considered abnormal. As a result, many youths get married who really don't want to, or even more common, they marry before they are personally ready to do so.

One of the things we know for certain is that those who marry in their middle or late twenties have about one third the divorce rate of those who marry in their teens (Rice, 1979, p. 68). For this reason alone, adults have to be careful not to pressure young people into relationships for which they are not ready, and to accept the fact that a small minority may never desire to get married at all. The important emphasis in the Christian religion is that individuals should feel free to choose the course they feel God desires of them. Achtemeier writes:

> God gives his own special gift and task to both married and unmarried . . . and finding the direction of one's life in the will of God gives one a marvelous freedom from Society's dictates as to what one ought or ought not to do. . . .
>
> Because the Christian gospel bestows the freedom to choose one's course, and because it founds that freedom on one's responsibility to God alone, it also follows that the gospel shows up inadequate reasons for marriage. (Achtemeier, 1976, p. 27)

MARRIAGE AS COMMITMENT AND RESPONSIBILITY

One important emphasis that is often lacking is the idea that successful marriage requires a complete *commitment* and tremendous *responsibility.* To marry a person means that one promises to love, cherish, and care for that person as an extension of one's self. It involves a promise, a vow that each makes to the other "before God and these witnesses." It involves entering into a covenant or an agreement to do certain things.

If I were to ask the average couple, "What promises did you make to each other, or what vows did you take when you got married?" chances are they could not tell me. In the excitement of getting married, people often overlook the content and meaning of their marital vows. Only afterward, when the full burden of responsibility falls upon them, do they wonder: "What have I done?"

Any religious rite is full of meaning and significance.

While the rites vary among different religious groups, there are some things they have in common. Four parties as represented in the marriage service: the couple, the religious group (minister), the state (witnesses), and the parents (usually through the father). Each party to the rite covenants with the others to fulfill its obligations so that marriage will be blessed "according to the ordinance of God and the law of the state." The church, through the minister, pledges God's grace, love, and blessing. The couple makes vows to each other "in the presence of God and these witnesses." The state grants the marriage license as proof that the requirements of the law have been fulfilled (the witnesses are present to see that the law is obeyed). The parents (through the father) pledge to give up their daughter to her new husband. In all of the services, the couples must indicate their willingness to be married: they make certain pledges to each other; they indicate to the minister their agreement to abide by divine ordinance and civil law; they join hands as a symbol of their new union (Rice, 1979, p. 173).

The minister usually asks the husband, then the wife:

> *N.*, wilt thou have this Woman (Man) to be thy wife (husband), and wilt thou pledge thy troth to her (him), in all love and honor, in all duty and service, in all faith and tenderness, to live with her (him), and cherish her (him), according to the ordinance of God, in the holy bond of marriage? (*The Book of Common Worship*, 1946, pp. 184f. The word "troth" means faithfulness.)

In response, the man, and then the woman, says: "I will." Then the minister asks: "Who giveth this woman to be married to this man?" The father responds: "I do," or "Her mother and I do." The father then places the hand of his daughter in that of the groom, no longer coming between them, and then sits back down beside his own wife. In accepting her hand in marriage, the groom then repeats the vows:

> I, *N.*, take thee, *N.*, to be my wedded wife, and I do promise and covenant, before God and these witnesses, to be thy loving and faithful husband, in plenty and in want, in joy and in sorrow, in sickness and in health, as long as we both shall live. (*The Book of Common Worship*, 1946, p. 185)

The bride then takes the hand of the groom, and repeats the same vow, after which the groom and bride each give and accept rings as a visible reminder of the promises made: "This ring I give thee, in token and pledge, of our constant faith, and abiding love." After prayer the minister concludes the service by pronouncing:

> By the authority committed unto me as a Minister of the Church of Christ, I declare that *N.* and *N.* are now Husband and Wife, according to the ordinance of God, and the law of the State: in the name of the Father, and of the Son, and of the Holy Spirit. Amen. (*The Book of Common Worship*, 1946, p. 187)

The husband and wife join their right hands, and the minister adds:

> Whom therefore God hath joined together, let no man put asunder. (*The Book of Common Worship*, 1946, p. 187)

In recent years, there has been a tendency for couples to write their own contract and vows, so that what is promised may differ from the traditional Protestant service, but the important emphasis remains that getting married implies making a commitment and a promise to keep it.

One of the things that I find lacking in many young people is this very concept that being a mature, Christian adult implies assuming responsibility. The other day a teenager told me, "I want my parents to treat me as an adult." But the parents replied, "She wants the privileges of adulthood but none of the responsibility." This was true. One young couple who came to me to be married had a superficial attitude toward the whole thing. They remarked, "Oh, if it doesn't work out, we'll get a divorce." Certainly, if they took their vows so lightly and refused to really work at making their marriage succeed, it is doubtful that it would work out. Marriage at its best requires sacrifices, motivation, courage, persistence, patience, a high level of unselfishness, loyalty, love, and devotion to each other, and sometimes even much self-sacrifice.

These things are required of both the husband and the wife. Research in marriage relationships has shown that far too often it is the wife who makes most of the sacrifices, that it is she who is most concerned about the quality of the relationship, and she who is most motivated to make it work. Too many husbands go to the altar and say "I do" and then turn over the task of marriage maintenance to their wives. They even turn over to their wives the task of raising the children, even if their wives work full-time outside the home. As a consequence, many wives feel used, abused, and overburdened, so that far greater numbers of wives are unhappy with their marriages than is true of husbands. In many cases the husbands have everything done for them, but do not assume their share of the burden at home. Such arrangements just don't work. Marriage success requires the best efforts of two people. One person acting alone can never make a marriage work. No one is ready for marriage who is not yet ready to bear his or her full share of the burden. "Bear one another's burdens, and so fulfil the law of Christ" (Gal. 6:2).

MARRIAGE AS AN EXCLUSIVE RELATIONSHIP

When people marry, they promise faithfulness and fidelity. Thus, the Jewish husband promises in the *ketubah:* "I faithfully promise that I will be a true husband unto thee" (Brill et al., 1973, p. 26). Thus, religious marriage is an *exclusive* relationship. According to one version of the marriage service, the bride and groom promise each other: "forsaking all others, to cling only to thee."

Most young people today accept this need for fidelity after marriage. A 1973 survey among young people showed that 60 percent of college students and 65 percent of noncollege youths said that they thought that extramarital sexual relations were wrong (Yankelovich, 1974, p. 91). This still leaves a significant proportion (40 and 35 percent respectively) who don't believe it is wrong, which make us wonder how many of these young people have no intention of remaining faithful to their mates after marriage.

In spite of the efforts of large numbers of writers to convince the public that anyone who demands sexual exclusiveness in marriage is "old fashioned," "jealous," "stilted," "unrealistic," or perpetuating "closed marriages," the overwhelming evidence is that adultery in any form, whether clandestine or by mutual permission of the married couple, is destructive to the marital relationship. (See my book *Sexual Problems in Marriage,* 1978, p. 136.)

A study by Frederick Humphrey, president of the American Association of Marriage and Family Counselors, showed that nearly half the cases brought to marriage counselors involved adultery (Humphrey, 1977). The situation was a particularly serious one, since one third of the couples in these cases planned to divorce because of the affair. In almost half the cases, the affair had been in progress for more than six months before help was sought. Humphrey found that the average couple were middle-class, had been married twelve years, and had at least one child (Humphrey, 1977).

Partly because of the frequent presentation of adulterous affairs in the mass media, there has been an increasing tendency to accept such behavior as a normal part of modern life. It is frequent, yes, but never should be accepted as normal, since it is harmful to truly meaningful, loving, committed, monogamous marriage. Keeping the commandment "You shall not commit adultery" is not only moral but necessary if marriage is to survive.

Youths who get married, therefore, have to be willing and ready to settle down with one person. This does not mean they give up all friends, but it means they agree to complete and total sexual exclusiveness. Those who feel compelled to "play the field" and to continue to "sow their wild oats" or "flit from flower to flower" are not mature or moral enough to make marriage work, and ought not to get married, or to be pressured by parents into getting married, at least not until they are more grown up, emotionally and spiritually.

MARRIAGE AS A GROWING RELATIONSHIP

Another important principle is that Christian marriage can never be a static relationship. It is a *growing*, changing relationship. Marriage is not something that happens once and for all; it is rather an ongoing process, a process of becoming one—united in spirit and under the Lordship of Christ. It is a process in which two persons achieve a unity of body, mind, and spirit.

This means that there is a difference between a wedding

ceremony and a marriage. This difference was recognized by a young husband-to-be who said, "We aren't going to have much of a wedding, but we are going to have a wonderful marriage." A wedding is a once-and-for-all thing that is quickly over, but once it is over the real marriage must begin. This process by which two separate, distinct individuals become united may take months or years. It begins when the couple first begin to share their bodies, their feelings, their home, their bed, their food, their work, their money, their social life, their ideas, their worship. The process never ends, for as the years pass and they find new things to share, the marriage bond tightens. There are some couples who are still finding ways to grow closer after many years of marriage.

Of course, the opposite can happen: they can grow apart, so that in an emotional and spiritual sense, even though not in a legal sense, the marriage has been broken and is ended. They are no longer united; they now go their separate ways as two persons.

It is important to recognize that, in the process whereby two become one, each person needs to keep his or her own identity. Marriage should not result in one person becoming completely absorbed, dominated, swallowed up by the other. Marriage does not destroy individual identity, but should fulfill it. Perhaps healthy and unhealthy relationships can be illustrated by the following diagrams. Diagram #1 shows a healthy relationship. The husband and wife are equals, but have achieved considerable unity in many areas of their personalities, so they can truly say they have partly become one physically, mentally, emotionally, socially, and spiritually. Diagrams #2 and #3 show unhealthy relationships. In diagram #2 one spouse has lost all identity because he or she has been dominated and absorbed by the other. In diagram #3 the relationship is one of unequals, where one person has become a satellite revolving around the other. And in diagram #4 the marriage is broken. There is no marriage, only two separate, unrelated, ununited people.

One of the problems young couples face is that they expect that they will be "married" all at once. They still confuse the marriage with the wedding, so when they have problems, they are dumbfounded that this should happen to them. Some become disillusioned and ready to give up because marriage is not quite what they expected. One answer is to help them have more realistic concepts of what marriage is and what it involves, and through appropriate premarital education and guidance to help them evaluate their relationship realistically to determine areas of agreement and disagreement, compatibility and incompatibility, so they will know ahead of time what areas they will have to work on to make their marriage more complete.

MARRIAGE AS A RELATIONSHIP OF EQUALS

There is a commonly held notion that the Christian religion teaches patriarchal domination of the husband over the wife. This is really not fair or true. Various Scripture passages do reflect the ancient and traditional Jewish attitude toward women. This attitude emphasized that sons were more desired than daughters; wives were subject to their husbands without having the same legal rights; husbands were to exercise rule over their wives; husbands could divorce their wives but not the other way around, and so on. There is no question that these attitudes are clearly reflected in the Old Testament. Achtemeier suggests, however, that in their original state, before the fall, the man and the woman enjoyed a completely equal

Figure 14-1

HEALTHY AND UNHEALTHY
MARRIAGE RELATIONSHIPS

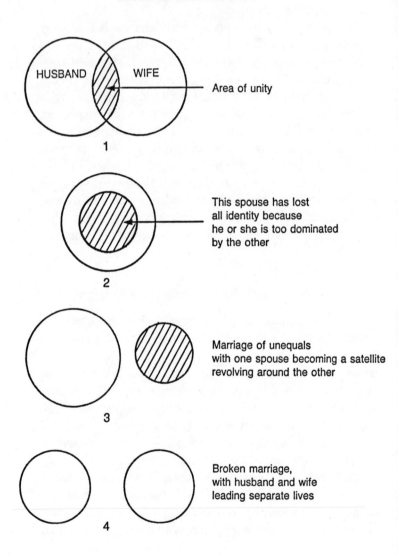

status, with the wife "corresponding" to the husband so that he recognized her as "bone of my bones and flesh of my flesh" (Gen. 2:23). The woman was made subject to her husband because of her sin, so that God said to her: "Your desire shall be for your husband, and he shall rule over you" (Gen. 3:16). Thus, the intended wholesomeness and equality of the relationship was disrupted because the man and the woman denied their subservience to God (Achtemeier, 1976, p. 74).

In the New Testament, however, all become reconciled to God through Christ, so that Paul could say "there is neither male nor female; for you are all one in Christ Jesus" (Gal. 3:28). "You were bought with a price; do not become slaves of men" (I Cor. 7:23). "For freedom Christ has set us free; stand fast, therefore, and do not submit again to a yoke of slavery" (Gal. 5:1). Paul is here talking about freedom from slavery to the law as interpreted minutely by Jewish legalism, but he is also emphasizing that Christ has died for all, and that all are equal in his sight. Certainly, Jesus made no distinction in his ministry between men and women; He served both and enlisted the help of both (Achtemeier, 1976, p. 76).

The important emphasis in the New Testament is that wives and husbands are commanded to serve one another. Thus, Paul said, "Be subject to one another out of reverence for Christ" (Eph. 5:21). Wives were to be subject to their husbands. Husbands were to love their wives as Christ loved his church (Eph. 5:22, 26). It is clear that the husband-wife relationship must be one of mutual subjection or of mutual giving. In the eyes of Jesus, those who desire to assume positions of leadership must also be willing to perform the greatest service. Jesus said, "Whoever would be great among you must be your servant, and whoever would be first among you must be slave of all"

(Mark 10:43, 44). True greatness and a position of leadership in the eyes of Jesus implies maximum service.

We cannot emphasize too much the importance of mutual servitude and subjection. It is always disastrous to marriage when one person does all the giving and the other does all the receiving. A person who does all the giving soon becomes physically, emotionally, and spiritually exhausted, and the one who does all the receiving is only being encouraged in tyranny.

One of the things that is happening in our modern culture is that women are seeking full and equal legal and civil rights to employment, income, and other privileges. This struggle has only been partially won outside the home. Women still are paid only 60 percent of the salary of men for comparable work, experience, and education. (For a full discussion see Rice, 1979, p. 220.) This struggle has also been only partly won in the home. Even though slightly over half of all married women work outside the home, and the majority of these have dependent children, these women, by and large, still bear the same burdens for homemaking, housekeeping, and caring for children in the home. What has happened is that women are sharing the task of providing income, but by and large their husbands have not assumed their fair share of the burden of homemaking and child-rearing. This fact has been well documented by research studies. Space permits only one example. One study by the U.S. Department of Agriculture gave a detailed analysis of what husbands and wives actually do around the house ("How Much Does He Do Around the House?" 1971). According to this study, husbands averaged a total of one and one half hours a day on yard and home care, car upkeep, food preparation or cleanup, taking care of children, and all home tasks combined. This was true regardless of whether the wife was a full-time homemaker or full-time job holder—thirty or more hours a week. Those women who were full-time job holders still spent an additional four and one half hours daily on homemaking tasks, or three times the amount of time spent by their husbands. This means that while egalitarian and democratic marriages emphasize that the husband and wife share everything 50-50, in actual practice the wife still takes the primary responsibility for housekeeping and child care. No wonder that so many working wives and mothers feel overburdened!

One researcher found that holding a full-time job plus meeting the family's domestic needs requires 105 hours a week (Howell, 1973). This means that if a woman tries to work full-time and take care of her family herself, without paid help or help from her husband or children, she will be working fifteen hours a day, seven days a week, more than the equivalent of two full-time jobs. Why should one member of the family have two jobs when no one else does? Certainly, the Christian concept of equality implies equal privileges and equal responsibilities.

MARRIAGE AS A PERMANENT RELATIONSHIP

Christian marriage is intended "till death do us part." "Whom therefore God hath joined together, let no man put asunder." Obviously, God's intention and present-day reality do not agree, since today about one third of all marriages are ending in divorce, with the rate climbing steadily (Rice, 1979, p. 457). The reasons for this are quite complicated (see Rice, 1979), but one fact remains: the Christian ideals of marriage are not being followed in day-to-day living, and whatever the reasons for divorce, increasing numbers of couples have to admit that their marriages have failed. This does not mean we should condemn these couples or ostracize them from the Christian community. Few people really want to get divorced. On the average, divorce occurs after seven years of marriage, and as the climax to years of hurt, misunderstanding, conflict, and unhappiness. Divorce occurs because people can't stand living together any longer! And they haven't been able to find solutions to their problems. In most cases, divorce is one of the most disturbing, upsetting experiences they will ever go through. Those who are so suffering need the help and assistance of the Christian community more than ever.

The New Testament teaches against divorce; there is no doubt about that (Matt. 19:6; Mark 10:2–9). Christ allowed one reason: that of unchastity (Matt. 5:32; 19:9). Some churches, following Paul, also allow the believer to divorce an unbelieving spouse if peace is not possible any other way (I Cor. 7:15). But according to Biblical teaching divorce is not God's will, even though allowed. "For your hardness of heart Moses allowed you to divorce your wives, but from the beginning it was not so" (Matt. 19:8). But we are cautioned also to avoid Biblical legalism, which places more emphasis on the letter of the law than the spirit behind it. Thus, we need to remember that according to the spirit of Jesus' teachings and in keeping with the principles of Christian love, divorce may at times be the most loving thing to do. Should a wife, for example, stay with an unbelieving husband who beats her and the children? Should a husband live a lifetime with an alcoholic wife who refuses to admit her problem and to seek help? Should a person live with another in a relationship of hate and rejection, where one person refuses to try to improve the relationship? In such cases, divorce may be the only merciful, loving thing to do.

But the point is, we have to teach our young people that

marriage is serious business, and whenever divorce is contemplated there should be compelling "Christian reasons for violating the intention of God" (Kee, 1957, p. 34). Young people who enter into marriage lightly or who contemplate divorce for superficial reasons and without making any real effort to make the marriage work are disobeying God's will. Those who truly seek to follow him will resolve to do all in their power to succeed. And certainly, sincere effort and strong motivation, along with seeking God's help, have enabled many couples to work through problems and to build a lasting and satisfying relationship.

15
Sexual Values and Behavior

A 1976 survey of young women ages 15 to 19 showed that one in five had had premarital sexual intercourse by age 16 (Zelnik et al., 1979, p. 182). Sixty percent had had premarital sexual intercourse by age 19. An estimated one in five of all young women in the United States become premaritally pregnant by 19 years of age. If just these women who are sexually active are considered, over one fifth become premaritally pregnant by age 16 and over one third by age 19.

When these data are compared with prior years, it becomes quite obvious that the percentages of young unmarried women who are having sexual intercourse is steadily increasing (Zelnik et al., 1979, p. 183). Since substantial numbers become pregnant, it is obvious that many are not using any reliable methods of birth control. In fact, national figures show that about one third of all teenagers who have sexual intercourse never use any method of contraception, over 40 percent indicate they only sometimes use contraceptives, and only about one in five indicate they use contraceptives every time they have intercourse (Zelnik and Kantner, 1978, p. 136).

The rising incidence of premarital sexual activity and pregnancy has stimulated thoughtful church leaders to reexamine many of their historic ethical positions about human sexuality to see if some of these views need to be revised in the light of present-day reality. I shall not attempt to summarize all the pros and cons of this discussion, but I do want to go back to Biblical teachings and then to examine these in the light of modern knowledge which has helped in the development of a Christian ethical position.

BIBLICAL TEACHINGS

Positive Attitudes

What does the Bible say about human sexuality? Most importantly, there is nothing repressive in the Biblical view of sex. The love poetry in the Song of Solomon is filled with sexual imagery:

> How graceful are your feet in sandals,
>   O queenly maiden!
> Your rounded thighs are like jewels,
>   the work of a master hand.
> Your navel is a rounded bowl
>   that never lacks mixed wine.
> Your belly is a heap of wheat,
>   encircled with lilies.
> Your two breasts are like two fawns,
>   twins of a gazelle.
>   (Song of Solomon 7:1–3)

In Gen. 18:12, Sarah speaks of sexual intercourse as pleasure, and the word comes from the same root as used for "Eden" or "paradise" (Achtemeier, 1976, p. 156). In the New Testament, Jesus says: "For this reason a man shall leave his father and mother and be joined to his wife, and the two shall become one flesh. So they are no longer two but one flesh" (Mark 10:7, 8). Certainly in this passage Jesus approves of sexual intercourse between two married people. One of Jesus' first acts in beginning his ministry was to attend a marriage feast at Cana (John 2:1–11).

There have been times in the history of the Christian church when it taught repressive, ascetic views of sex. Sex was looked upon as necessary for procreation but quite evil otherwise. Augustine, for example, voiced the opinion that he wished the Creator had contrived some other way that children could be conceived (Bainton, 1957). But modern theologians regard such attitudes as unbiblical and unchristian and contrary to the intentions of God. A 1977 volume entitled *Human Sexuality: New Directions in American Catholic Thought* says that "Christians must be encouraged to embrace their sexuality joyfully and in full consciousness" (Catholic Theological Society of America, 1977). This attitude closely reflects the Biblical witness and is a drastic change from the negative teachings of the church a generation or so ago.

Forbidden Expressions

Of course, not all types of sexual expression may be regarded as vital and good. The Bible, and especially the New Testament, specifically teaches against:

Adultery—See Ex. 20:14; Lev. 20:10; Deut. 5:18; Matt. 15:19; Gal. 5:19.

Prostitution—See Prov. 7; I Cor. 6:15, 16.

Incest—See Lev. 18:6–18; 20:11–21; I Cor. 5:1.

Bestiality (sexual intercourse with an animal)—See Lev. 18:23; 20:15; Deut. 27:21.

Homosexuality—See Lev. 18:22; 20:13; Deut. 23:17, 18; Rom. 1:24–27; I Cor. 6:9, 10.

Fornication (unchastity, which can mean both premarital sexual intercourse and sex with prostitutes)—See Acts 15:20: Col. 3:5, 6; I Thess. 4:3.

Because of its importance, a whole section of this chapter will be devoted to the subject of fornication.

There have been some efforts to teach that the Bible forbids masturbation, but this is based upon one vague reference to Onan in Gen. 38:1–11. When Onan's brother died, he was expected to perform the duty of a brother-in-law by sleeping with his ex-brother's wife, but he knew the offspring would not be his; so when he went in to the woman "he spilled the semen on the ground, lest he should give offspring to his brother" (Gen. 38:9). The Biblical writer goes on to say that this was displeasing to the Lord, so the Lord slew him (Gen. 38:10). But it is not clear by what means Onan spilled his seed: whether by *masturbation* or by *coitus interruptus* (Cole, 1959, pp. 297, 374). Since neither of these are anywhere mentioned in the New Testament, to try to make either one sinful on the basis of Biblical teaching is certainly far-fetched. Certainly masturbation is so prevalent among adolescents as to be considered universally practiced. And practically all competent health, medical, and psychiatric authorities now say that masturbation is a normal part of growing up and does not have, in and of itself, any harmful physical or mental effects, nor does it in any way interfere with normal sexual adjustment in marriage. In fact, masturbation seems to be beneficial in achieving orgasm during intercourse. The only ill effect of masturbation comes not from the act itself, but from the guilt, fear, or anxiety that comes from the adolescent believing the practice will do harm (Rice, 1978, pp. 380, 381) The best thing that adults and parents can do about masturbation is nothing, or to relieve anxiety and guilt about it if such are found. If, however, the adolescent masturbates to the exclusion of normal friendships and social activities, he or she has a problem, not with masturbation, but with social adjustments, and the parent should be concerned about these. In this case, masturbation is a symptom of social maladjustment, not a cause (Rice, 1978, p. 382). I don't feel we have any valid grounds for teaching our young people that it is a sin.

SEX AS GOOD OR EVIL

We must also avoid labeling sexual actions and activities as good or bad strictly on the basis of overt acts. After all, sex involves feelings, motivations, and relationships, so that the context in which behavior is expressed may be as important in judging morality as the activities themselves. What I'm saying is that sex is intended as a good, but can become corrupted so as to be an evil. For example, sex is intended as an expression of love in the marriage relationship, but it can also be used before or after marriage in immoral ways. Those ways include:

Sex as *punishment.* A teenage girl is angry at her parents, so she deliberately gets pregnant to get back at them. Or, a husband is angry at his wife, so forces intercourse upon her in a rough, uncaring way.

Sex as an *escape.* A teenage girl gets pregnant so she can escape from an unhappy home situation.

Sex as a means of *exploitation.* A young man seeks sexual partners to use to satisfy his lust without regard for their feelings or the consequences of his actions.

Sex as a *payment.* A boy takes a girl to dinner and a movie, and afterward expects intercourse in return for what he has done. "What do I get after I spent all that money?" is really the prostitution of sex. Or, a girl exchanges sexual favors for new clothes or other gifts.

Sex as a means of *controlling behavior.* "I won't sleep

with you unless you do as I say." I know one underage couple that wanted to get married, but their parents wouldn't give permission. "I'll get pregnant and then they'll sign" was the girl's attitude. She did get pregnant, and the parents did sign. Or, how many girls get pregnant deliberately to try to get the boy to marry them? This is using sex to try to control the behavior of other persons.

Sex as a *means of building one's ego* because of neurotic need. There is the Don Juan who tries to seduce as many girls as possible to build up his own ego. Or, there are girls who satisfy a neurotic need to feel loved by seeking sexual relations. One girl who had become pregnant twice out of wedlock remarked: "At least I feel loved while it's happening." Actually, this wasn't love, it was exploitation.

Sex as a *means of conceiving an illegitimate child.* Any irresponsible use of sex that conceives a child that cannot be cared for properly, in marriage, is a sinful use of what was intended as a good.

What I'm saying is that sometimes sex is not completely right or wrong in and of itself. It can be a good or an evil. There are many things in life like that. Alcohol used medicinally is a good, but when used in alcoholic beverages and drunk in excess, it can completely destroy human lives. Parents and teachers need to teach youths to use sex lovingly, responsibly, to help rather than to hurt.

PREMARITAL SEXUAL BEHAVIOR

The most difficult questions relate to sexual expression before marriage. Is sexual expression ever "right" before marriage according to Christian teachings? We have to recognize that very deep-thinking, sincere Christians do differ on what they feel is acceptable and unacceptable behavior. This means that sincere, responsible young people can probably find some church support for whatever reasonable views they are able to accept themselves. To be specific, there are sincere Christians who feel that premarital sexual intercourse between two people who love each other and who are committed to each other to get married sometime in the future is right and good. There are other sincere Christians who accept complete sexual abstinence as the only standard for them. Who is right? On the basis of Biblical teaching, abstinence is the preferred standard, since the Scriptures, and especially the New Testament, exhort Christians to avoid all *porneia* which is variously translated fornication, unchastity, or immorality (meaning sexual immorality) (Acts. 15:20; Col. 3:5, 6; I Thess. 4:3). Thus, Paul wrote to the Thessalonians:

> For you know what instructions we gave you through the Lord Jesus. For this is the will of God, your sanctification: that you abstain from unchastity; that each one of you know how to take a wife for himself in holiness and honor, not in the passion of lust like heathen who do not know God; that no man transgress, and wrong his brother in this matter, because the Lord is an avenger in all these things, as we solemnly forewarned you. For God has not called us for uncleanness, but in holiness. Therefore whoever disregards this, disregards not man but God, who gives his Holy spirit to you. (I Thess. 4:2–8)

The Scriptures are quite realistic about human sexual drives. The apostle Paul says: "Because of the temptation to immorality *(porneia)*, each man should have his own wife and each woman her own husband." And of the unmarried and widows he says: "If they cannot exercise self-control, they should marry. For it is better to marry than to be aflame with passion" (I Cor. 7:2, 9). In the Old Testament, if a man met a virgin who was not betrothed and lay with her, and they were discovered, the man had to pay her father fifty shekels of silver (the acceptable price for a bride) and, at the father's request, marry her because he had violated her. He could then never divorce her as long as he lived (Deut. 22:28, 29). If the father chose not to marry his daughter to her seducer, he had the alternative of keeping her at home, but could still collect the "money equivalent to the marriage present for virgins" (Ex. 22:16, 17). If, however, a man lay with a woman who was betrothed to another man, the penalty for him was death (Deut. 22:23–27).

The only possible circumstance in which a couple could engage in voluntary fornication was if they were betrothed. Since in the Old Testament betrothal was tantamount to marriage, the law was abolutely silent on sexual relations between a betrothed couple; no prohibition was set up and no punishments were provided (Cole, 1959, p. 235). It must be emphasized, however, that betrotral was *not* an informal understanding to marry, it was an agreement to marry. Cancellation of this agreement was unthinkable. The early Jews had no religious or civil ceremony of marriage. After the betrothal was arranged between the two sets of parents, and after a wedding feast, the groom went to the dwelling of his wife and brought her home with him.

If we were to go by the Old Testament alone, premarital sexual relations after formal engagement would be permitted. But this would have to be a complete and irreversible commitment to marriage. However, on the basis of the New Testament, all premarital sexual relations are forbidden. Couples should wait until after marriage.

What about the various degrees of sexual intimacy short of intercourse? The Bible is completely silent on such matters as necking and petting, so we have to use common sense and good judgment. I've always told youths that it is unfair and unrealistic to engage in intimate petting that is intended to stimulate sexual feelings, to prepare for intercourse, knowing that unchastity itself is forbidden. As far as I can determine, the "technical virgins" who pet to orgasm, who engage in every intimacy except actual coitus, are unchaste, and that such activity is forbidden in the New Testament.

I would, however, agree with the Biblical witness that there are degrees of sexual sinfulness. In my book *The Adolescent* (Rice, 1978, p. 367) I outline seven different standards of sexual permissiveness that are presently accepted, each by some person or group in our society. Those standards are:

> Abstinence
> The double standard
> Sex with affection, commitment, and responsibility
> Sex with affection and commitment, but without responsibility
> Sex with affection
> Sex without affection
> Sex with ulterior motives

I would immediately eliminate the last four standards and the double standard as unchristian. To engage in sex for ulterior motives, without affection, or without assuming responsibility for oneself, the other person, and one's actions is completely contrary to Christian ethical principles. Or to engage in sex, even with affection, but without commitment, is unchristian. And while the Old Testament recognizes a double standard, one for men and another for women, this is contrary to the spirit of the New Testament and must be rejected. This leaves only two standards: abstinence, and sex with affection, commitment, and responsibility. Abstinence is considered the Christian ideal prior to marriage and is strongly urged both in the New Testament and by most churches. Sex, even with affection, commitment, and responsibility, but before marriage, is accepted in the Old Testament but not in the New. If premarital intercourse is permitted at all on the basis of Old Testament teachings, it would have to be only after formal engagement and just prior to marriage, but since unchastity before marriage is clearly forbidden in the New Testament, and since the New Testament, not the Old Testament, is the standard for Christians, premarital sexual intercourse seems contrary to both the spirit and the letter of New Testament morality.

SOME CONTEMPORARY TRENDS

Unfortunately, present practice does not even approach the Christian ideal. In fact, we are witnessing some trends that are both unwise and immoral.

1. There is a trend among youths to engage in recreational sex. I am perplexed by the large numbers of young people who will go to bed with partners whom they have just met and scarcely know. Such relationships can't possibly be meaningful, and make sex a superficial experience. And what lacks meaning and is superficial eventually becomes dissatisfying and even distasteful. I've talked with young people who are shocked by their own behavior, and who feel quite "dirty" after spending the night with someone they didn't even care about, much less love.

2. There is increasing pressure on youths to "go all the way" because "everyone is doing it" or because "the guys expect it." Why should adolescents feel forced to have sex they don't really want, or sometimes don't even enjoy? More and more, the girls are saying: "All the guys expect you to sleep with them or they won't even take you out."

It is a deplorable situation for any girl to begin to feel that the only way she can get a date is to become promiscuous. Fortunately, not all youths are "doing it." It takes a great deal of courage to abide by one's own standards, but adults need to help their young people to have the courage to stand by their own convictions. It's the only way they can keep their own integrity and self-respect as human beings.

3. There is a continuing trend to show complete irresponsibility about preventing premarital pregnancy. One study among undergraduate college students showed that 45 percent of the males and 21 percent of the females expect their date to come equipped with contraceptives. If the male has not taken precautions, only 7 percent will ask the girl if she has. If neither person has taken precautions, 60 percent of the males and 34 percent of the females will go right ahead without any effective method (Bender, 1973). No wonder there are increasing numbers of premarital pregnancies among teenagers—now over a million a year (Westoff, 1976)! These pregnancies now result in over 200,000 illegitimate babies born each year to girls 15 to 19 years old, and over 300,000 abortions each year among this age group (Westoff, 1976; Forrest et al., 1978).

4. There is a trend for increasing numbers of youths to live together prior to marriage. These youths live together for various reasons, with different meanings attached to the relationships. In general, this kind of relationship may be divided up into five basic types:

The convenient, temporary, transient relationship without commitment. This type is in the minority and may be with or without sexual intimacy. The motive may be for practical reasons: to save money, to share an apartment, etc.

An intimate involvement with emotional commitment.

The couple say they are in love but have no permanent, long-range plans for marriage. This category includes the majority of college couples who are cohabiting.

A nonlegal, voluntary substitute for marriage. Such relationships involve only a minority of persons, but consist of those who feel that marriage is unnecessary, or destructive to love and intimacy, or who for one reason or another don't want to make a legal commitment.

A testing ground for marriage, or as a trial marriage. The couple are highly committed to each other and want to live together to determine the advisability of marriage.

A logical step before marriage. The couple are completely committed to one another and to marriage and are living together in the interim until marriage can be formalized.

From the best information that we now have available, there is no evidence that nonmarital cohabitation is good preparation for marriage, that couples who have cohabited prior to marriage are more happily married than those who have not, or that cohabitation is an improved method of mate selection. (See Rice, 1979, pp. 141–166.) So even among those who cohabit because they desire better marriages, there is no evidence that cohabitation will enable them to succeed.

As a marriage and family life educator and counselor, I welcome the trend among youths to marry at older ages. This fact should improve the quality of marriage because the people are more mature when they enter into the relationship. But, as far as I know, the only way to make an intelligent choice of mate is to get to know many persons as friends so that one can begin to judge what type of person one wants and should marry, and then to get to know a prospective partner well over a long period of time before commitment and marriage. This can be done without living together and without having intercourse. In fact, sex, or intimate living together, often confuses young people, or pressures them into marrying when they really are incompatible. Certainly the primary reason for marriage while in the teens is premarital pregnancy, which is the worst circumstance under which to marry.

It is quite evident that Christian idealism and present practice are quite different. Once the present trend toward promiscuity has run its course, it is quite likely that our society may return to a more sober, reasonable, and moral point of view. At the present time I feel that premarital sexual intercourse has created more problems than it has solved, both for our society and for individuals. For that reason, I do not agree that it can be adopted wholeheartedly as the new Christian ethic.

16
Drug Abuse*

Parents and other thinking adults have become alarmed at the increasing numbers of their young people who are turning to various kinds of drugs. The drugs most commonly abused may be grouped into a number of categories: *narcotics, stimulants, depressants, hallucinogens, marijuana,* and *inhalants. Alcohol* and *nicotine* are also drugs, and since they are more widely used than any of the others they will be discussed under separate sections of this chapter.

Narcotics

Narcotics include *opium* and its derivatives such as *morphine, heroin,* and *codeine.* These drugs are powerful depressants which act on the central nervous system. An overdose, especially when combined with alcohol, barbiturates, or other depressants can cause death. Narcotics are the most physically addictive of all drugs. Users

---

*Portions of this chapter were taken from F. Philip Rice, *The Adolescent: Development, Relationships, and Culture,* 2d ed. Copyright © 1978 by Allyn and Bacon, Inc., Boston. Reprinted with permission.

quickly develop a psychological dependence as well. This fact makes it most difficult for addicts to kick the habit, so the prognosis for curing well-established addiction is poor.

Stimulants

Cocaine is classified as a narcotic by federal law, so its use carries the same stiff penalties as narcotics, but it is a stimulant rather than a depressant to the central nervous system. Physical dependence is slight, but cocaine addiction can lead to a severe psychosis. Psychological dependence is severe, and withdrawal results in depression, which can only be relieved by more cocaine. Once well established, the compulsion to continue to use the drug is strong. The drug is usually sniffed, but may be injected.

Amphetamines (or "uppers") are stimulants and include such drugs as *Benzedrine, Dexedrine, Diphetamine,* and *Methedrine* (speed). Users soon develop a psychological need to continue taking the drugs. Mental depression and fatigue are experienced after withdrawal and psychic dependence develops quickly. The drugs are usually taken orally but when injected intravenously are among the most dangerous drugs used. Injection of Methedrine (speed) can cause rupture of the blood vessels and death. Heavy users often become violent, paranoid, or suicidal.

Depressants

Barbiturates are depressants (or "downers") which decrease the activity of the central nervous system. They include drugs commonly used in sleeping pills such as *Nembutal, Seconal, Amytal,* or *phenobarbital.* When used medicinally, as prescribed, they are safe, but when abused they are dangerous since they develop total addiction: physical and psychological dependence. Abusers who attempt to withdraw develop severe withdrawal symptoms. Fatal convulsions are a real danger. Delirium and hallucinations may develop.

Tranquilizers such as *Miltown, Equanil, Placidyl, Librium,* and *Valium* are also sedatives and, when abused, have the same dangers as barbiturates.

Hallucinogens

Hallucinogens or *psychedelic* drugs include a broad range of substances: *LSD, peyote, mescaline, PCP, STP* or *DOM, DMT,* and *MDA.* In general, the drugs alter perception and the state of consciousness, including the distortion of color, sound, time, and speed, and are quite unpredictable in their results because such minute quantities are so strong, and because most of the drugs are homemade with doses unknown. Some users report "bad trips" that are characterized by terror, panic, and psychosis. Users have been driven to suicide, violence, murder, or psychosis. These drugs, and especially LSD, must be viewed with extreme suspicion since brain damage and chromosomal alterations are possible.

Marijuana

Marijuana or *cannabis* is now very widely abused by young people. The drug is an intoxicant with the effect depending upon the THC content. *Hashish,* or *hashish oil,* is made from resin extracted from female flowers and contain the highest THC content. Physical dependency does not occur in users taking small or weak amounts, but it can develop with high dose administration so that sudden discontinuance can cause withdrawal symptoms. The development of psychological dependency is common, so that chronic users find it difficult to break the habit.

Is marijuana harmful? Evidence is mounting that what many youths considered harmless is certainly not, particularly when used regularly and in heavy concentrations. Some harmful effects of prolonged and chronic use may include the following:

1. Reduction of the level of the male hormone, testosterone, in the blood stream with possible decrease in sexual drive and an increase in impotence in males. While clearcut cause and effect have not been established, the suspicion is growing that marijuana plays an important part in this problem.

2. Lung irritation and disease. One marijuana cigarette has as many carcinogens (cancer-producing agents) as twenty tobacco cigarettes, so chronic users run the risk of developing the same lung problems as chronic tobacco users.

3. Psychosis can occur under conditions of unusually heavy use.

4. Heavy and prolonged use diminishes intellectual performance, motivation, and interest in work and in other conventional activities. So-called "burn-outs" may now be found in every junior high school, high school, and college. This happens in youths who use marijuana so heavily that normal functioning and motivation to do day-by-day work are impossible.

5. Intoxication impairs memory, alters the time sense, and reduces performance ability in a variety of tasks, making driving while under the influence very hazardous.

6. Marijuana use causes an increase in heart rate, so that it decreases exercise tolerance of those with heart disease. Thus, use by those with cardiovascular disease is most unwise.

Inhalants

The solvent fumes from plastic glue, gasoline, paint thinner, and hydrocarbons are sniffed to give an intoxicating effect. Blurring of vision, ringing ears, slurred speech, and staggering are common, followed by drowsiness, stupor, and even unconsciousness. Deaths from glue-sniffing have occurred because of suffocation while the plastic bag is over the head, or because of accidents like falling from high places. Severe organ damage to kidneys, liver, heart, blood, and nervous system remain a possibility.

REASONS FOR USING

Beginning Use

Why do so many youths use drugs? The overwhelming majority try drugs out of curiosity to see what they are like. Adolescents have heard about different drugs and decide to try them. If they are more attracted by the promises of a drug than by its potential harm, they may be led to experiment.

Another reason for trying drugs is for fun or sensual pleasure. They do it "just for kicks" because they are seeking excitement.

Another strong motive is the social pressure to be like friends or to be a part of a social group. "My friends urged me to try it, and I didn't want to be chicken" is commonly heard. This motive is especially strong in immature youths who are seeking group approval.

One important motive for trying drugs is to relieve tensions, anxieties, or pressures, to escape from problems or to be able to deal with them or to face them.

"I needed to get away from the problems that have been bothering me."

"I felt tired and needed a lift."

"I had to stay awake to study for exams."

Those who use drugs as an escape from tension, anxiety,

problems, or reality, or to make up for personal inadequacies are likely to become chronic users. These are the insecure, dependent persons who find that life is too much and who turn to drugs for relief or help.

Chronic Use

Adolescents who use addictive drugs may develop a physical addiction without meaning to and find themselves unable to stop. Those who use nonaddictive drugs as a means of trying to solve emotional problems become psychologically dependent upon them. Drugs become a means for finding security, comfort, or relief. Chronic users often come from disturbed or broken family situations where they have had problems getting along with their parents. The net effect of these types of family environments has been to create personality problems that cause individuals to turn to drugs as a consequence. Chronic users are often those who lack the inner resources to deal with their anxieties, tensions, fears, and confusion about their identity and values. Unable to rely on early family relationships or present friendships for help, they turn to drugs to lessen the pain and conflict and as a substitute for meaningful human relationships.

Sources of Supply

Youths report little difficulty in obtaining drugs. When they first try any drug, they usually obtain it as a gift from a friend. Thereafter, they usually purchase the drug from a friend, receive it as a gift, or find a person who is a dealer, and buy from that individual. Stimulants, sedatives, and opiates are often obtained from a person's own prescription or from forged prescriptions. Sedatives, heroin, and other opiates are the drugs most frequently stolen, primarily because they are physically addicting.

Studies refute the common stereotype of sinister adult drug pushers hanging around schools to persuade innocent youths to try "dope." Most commonly, students obtain drugs from a best friend or school classmate, or occasionally from dropouts who come on school grounds to sell drugs.

ALCOHOL

Alcohol continues to be the preferred drug among all elements of our society, including young people. At the present time, a substantial proportion of adolescents drink alcoholic beverages. Figure 16-1 shows the percentage of teenagers in 1974 who had ever had a drink. Note that the percentage increases with each school grade (Rice, 1978, p. 173).

But it is not just drinking as such, but frequent, excessive drinking which creates problems. At the present time, about one in twenty junior or senior high students are problem drinkers (Rice, 1978, p. 173). About 60 percent of seniors in high school get drunk at least once a month (Swift, 1975). About 10 percent get drunk once a week or more. The use of alcohol among girls has now begun to approach that of boys.

Adolescents drink for a number of reasons. Drinking is a widespread adult custom and the habits of adolescents reflect their perception of the attitudes and behavior of adults. Some adolescents use alcohol because they want to act "grown up" and they consider drinking as their "rite of passage" into the adult community. Youths also drink because of peer-group pressure and the need for peer identification, sociability, and friendship.

Another reason youths drink is as a means of rebellion.

Figure 16-1

PERCENTAGE OF TEENAGERS WHO HAVE EVER HAD
A DRINK OF WINE, BEER, OR SPIRITS
(BY SCHOOL GRADE AND SEX, U.S.A. 1974)

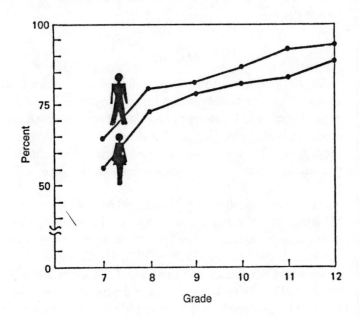

From U.S. Department of Health, Education, and Welfare. Public Health
Service. *Alcohol and Health*. Second Report to the U.S. Congress, 1974
(National Institute on Alcohol Abuse and Alcoholism, 1975), p. 8.

This is especially true of problem drinkers. They drink in defiance of parental authority or community norms as a way of expressing their hostility toward those in authority. The greater the rebellion, the greater the chance that the adolescent will become a problem drinker.

Problem drinkers drink to excess for psychological rather than social reasons. If drinking becomes heavy, it is often symptomatic of personality problems. Problem drinkers among youths are those with problems. They often don't get along at home, or at school. They may be receiving poor grades, are often delinquency prone, and often have disturbed relationships with parents.

SMOKING

Today over half of all junior high school students and two thirds of all senior high youths have smoked. More than half of all youths who smoke have their first cigarette before age twelve; 85 percent who smoke do so by age fifteen. This high incidence of smoking continues in spite of the fact that most youths are aware of the dangers.

There are many reasons for young people smoking. Certainly they are brainwashed from the early years of childhood by advertising that makes smoking synonymous with masculinity, female independence, nature, athletic prowess, beauty, sex, intelligence, sex appeal, sociability, wealth, and the good life. The sultry woman's voice, the social or back-to-nature setting, the tattooed hairy hands, all promise rewards the teenager seeks.

Youths also start for other reasons: they imitate parents and other adults who smoke. They start because of peer-group pressure. Smoking is often linked to the need for self-esteem and for status among some youths. Once youths start smoking they find it harder and harder to break the habit. It has been found, for example, that tobacco is physically addictive, as well as developing psychological dependency, so these factors together account for the fact that some people are not able to quit, even though they want to and try.

Drug Education and Prevention

One answer to the drug and tobacco problem is to try to keep adolescents from starting in the first place. A number of studies have been conducted to determine the most effective way to do this (Rice, 1978, pp. 171, 172). The following points are significant.

Drug education should avoid scare tactics that attempt to frighten adolescents. It is all right to point to the facts. Anxiety about harmful effects, to a degree, can be helpful in preventing adolescents from starting or in motivating them to stop. But scare tactics may lead adolescents to deny that there is danger of real harm, thus rejecting the teachings of the person who is trying to scare them.

Adolescents should be told all the facts as honestly as possible. Drug education and parental instruction should avoid half-truths and distortion of facts and make every effort to avoid a credibility gap. If adolescents find out that what adults tell them is not true, then they end up rejecting everything.

The primary appeal to young people should be positive. Instruction should appeal to their vanity, their pride, their belief in themselves and their sense of self-worth. They should be encouraged to take pride in their own physical fitness and mental alertness. Many a young person has refused drugs because he or she wanted to "stay in shape," or because of a desire to participate in athletics, or to take care of his or her body.

Religious parents should base part of their teaching on moral grounds. Paul writes to the Corinthians:

"All things are lawful for me," but not all things are helpful. "All things are lawful for me," but I will not be enslaved by anything. "Food is meant for the stomach and the stomach for food"—and God will destroy both one and the other. The body is not meant for immorality, but for the Lord, and the Lord for the body. . . . Shun immorality. Every other sin which a man commits is outside the body; but the immoral man sins against his own body. Do you not know that your body is a temple of the Holy Spirit within you, which you have from God? You are not your own; you were bought with a price. So glorify God in your body. (I Cor. 6:12, 13, 18–20)

Thus the old admonition to take care of your body because it is a temple of the Holy Spirit (I Cor. 6:19) has a continuing strong appeal to youths today. And the commandment "You shall not kill" (Ex. 20:13) applies as much to our own lives as it does to the lives of others. We are not to do anything to harm our own lives, and the implied converse commandment is that we are to do everything possible to preserve our lives.

Any instruction or educational program, to be effective, must begin when children are young and continue periodically over a span of years. Ten percent of the children in the United States, for example, are regular smokers by the age of twelve. This means that drug abuse education must begin by about the fourth or fifth grade.

Adults ought also to be alert for problems of emotional or social maladjustment that, if left unsolved, may lead to drug abuse. Thus, parents, teachers, and other adults should not hesitate to get counseling or guidance for all children as soon as needed. If the proper help is obtained at the right time, many problems can be prevented.

Adults need to recognize that if they don't want adolescents to smoke, drink, or use other drugs, they need to refrain from doing so themselves, since adolescents often imitate the example set in adult society by grown-ups. Also, if society does not want adolescents to use tobacco, alcohol, or other drugs, it needs to quit brainwashing them into believing that such things are synonymous with the "good life." Certainly drug abuse is a problem, but one that is created by a society that pushes drugs onto children and then condemns them if they get "hung up." Parents and other adults should use their influence to outlaw advertising that encourages young people to become abusers of substances that ultimately create much havoc.

17
Juvenile Crime and Delinquency*

The Delinquent

Terminology

The term *juvenile delinquency* refers to the violation of the law by a juvenile, which in most states means anyone under 18 years of age. A young person may be labeled a delinquent for breaking any one of a number of laws. The offense may be anything from murder and armed robbery to running away from home or truancy from school. As with adults, many crimes adolescents commit are never discovered or, if discovered, are not reported or prosecuted. Most statistics, therefore, underestimate the extent of juvenile crime.

Incidence

After remaining fairly constant for about five years, the rate of juvenile delinquency has begun to climb once more. At the present time, a little over one fourth of all persons arrested are juveniles under age 18, and an additional 31 percent are ages 18 to 24. Thus, over half of all

*Portions of this chapter were taken from F. Philip Rice, *The Adolescent: Development, Relationships, and Culture,* 2d ed. Copyright © 1978 by Allyn and Bacon, Inc., Boston. Reprinted with permission.

arrests are of people under age 25. The rate of delinquency among males is about three and one half times that among females of the same age, although the rate is increasing faster for girls than for boys.

TYPES OF CRIMES

The largest single category of crimes committed by both males and females is that of crimes against property—primarily theft. So-called victimless crimes include violations of drug or liquor laws, drunkenness, driving while intoxicated, gambling, prostitution, possessing illegal weapons, disorderly conduct, and vagrancy. These crimes constitute the second largest category of crimes committed by juveniles. Crimes against people include assault, rape, murder, manslaughter, sex offenses other than prostitution, and offenses against family or children.

The Bureau of the Census also groups eight major crimes together as "serious crimes." These crimes include larceny, burglary, motor vehicle theft, adultery, aggravated assault, forcible rape, murder, and manslaughter by negligence. One of the disturbing facts is that this group of crimes continues to increase faster than any other. For example, between 1970 and 1975

Murder committed by juvenile males increased	25%
Murder committed by juvenile females increased	56%
Forcible rape committed by juvenile males increased	17%
Forcible rape committed by juvenile females increased	4,800%
Aggravated assault committed by juvenile males increased	53%

Aggravated assault committed by juvenile
females increased   80%

Such a rapid increase in these more violent and serious crimes has caused considerable concern among authorities. The only category of serious crime committed by juvenile males that showed a decline between 1970 and 1975 was motor vehicle theft, with the incidence decreasing by 20 percent. However, motor vehicle theft by juvenile females increased 13 percent during the same period. (U.S. Department of Commerce, *Statistical Abstract of the United States,* 1976, Table No. 272.)

CAUSES OF DELINQUENCY

Concern over the increasing incidence of delinquency has led thinking people to try to determine the causes. Why do so many youths commit crimes? In general, the causes may be grouped into four major categories: *sociological factors,* which include social influences in our society; *psychological factors,* which include the influences of inner emotions, feelings, and personality components; *biological factors,* which include the effects of organic and physical elements; and *moral factors,* which include such things as the extent of moral education, the degree of involvement of the superego, and the opportunities for moral learning that have been offered to children.

Sociological Factors

The most important sociological factors in delinquency include at least seven elements.

Socioeconomic status and class have been found to be less important in relation to delinquency than was once thought. Traditionally, delinquency was thought to be a by-product of poverty. Recent investigations have revealed, however, that delinquency is becoming more widespread among all socioeconomic levels, although, when apprehended, middle-class youths are less often arrested and punished than those from poor families.

Affluence and hedonistic values and life-styles among modern youths contribute to delinquent behavior. Young people have cars, alcohol, drugs, and pocket money, and are involved in a whirl of social activities, often during late hours. These facts contribute to their getting into trouble.

Peer-group involvement becomes a significant factor in delinquency. Adolescents who spend a great deal of time hanging around with friends, especially with the wrong kind, are likely to get into trouble. *Neighborhood and community influences* are also important. Most cities have high crime areas which exert an influence on the behavior of youths in those areas.

Rapid social and cultural change stimulate anxiety and rebellion and a rejection of traditional values, which in turn increases delinquency rates.

The *level of school performance* is also related to delinquency. Lack of school success, classroom misconduct, difficulties in adjusting to school, administrators, and teachers, are all related to delinquency.

Family background is important. One study showed that children from broken homes are more than twice as likely to be charged with offenses as those from happy, unbroken homes (Chilton and Markle, 1972).

Psychological Factors

It is quite obvious that broken homes contribute toward delinquency, but often unhappy, disturbed family relationships exert just as negative an influence, even though the homes are not yet broken. Adolescents' relationships with their fathers are particularly important. Delinquents often describe their fathers as cold, punitive, unloving, unemotional, rejecting, neglectful, mistrusting, and lacking in understanding. Discipline is likely to be too hard, inconsistent, or nonexistent. The incidence of alcoholism is high.

Efforts have been made to discover personality traits or types that may be associated with delinquency. No one such personality type exists. In other words, not all delinquents are the same type of people, but many are described as socially assertive, defiant, resentful, hostile, suspicious, destructive, impulsive, and lacking in self-control. They consistently show low self-esteem and a negative self-image, and see themselves as "lazy," "bad," or "dumb." Thus, delinquency sometimes becomes an overcompensation for feelings of inferiority, rejection, or frustration. It is often a symptom of neurotic fears, anxieties, and hostilities.

Biological Factors

Organic or biological factors can be contributing causes to delinquency. For example, some delinquents show an incomplete development of the frontal lobe of the brain. Chromosomal aberrations may be the cause of aggressiveness, impulsiveness, and explosive, undisciplined behavior. Even such factors as low blood sugar, hearing impairments, hyperthyroidism, or brain damage may have some influence. Therefore, parents and teachers should have delinquent adolescents checked for physical problems before environmental or psychological causes are suspected.

Moral Factors

Some children get involved in delinquent acts not because of deep-seated psychological or physical problems, but simply as a result of the lack of moral education. They have not been taught right from wrong, so the conscience has not been developed sufficiently to act as a reliable guide to proper behavior. Over-indulged, undisciplined adolescents who have never been guided or controlled properly grow up believing that anything they do is all right. They commit minor offenses and are caught, and this becomes the beginning of a series of delinquent acts that get them deeper into trouble. Or, even more often, the moral examples set for them by parents and others are completely negative, so they learn to become criminals by identifying with their own parents.

THE TREATMENT OF JUVENILE OFFENDERS

The Police

The first contact that any adolescent has with the juvenile justice system is with the police. The police perform the function of maintaining and enforcing the law, but adolescents complain that the police do so differentially. For one thing, some police do "pick on kids." They arrest adolescents but let adults go for the same offense. Or, police arrest youths from the "wrong side of town," but overlook the behavior of youths from wealthy families. One of the reasons adolescents become bitter and cynical toward the police is the practice of unfair treatment or harassment by the police. Communities need to hire special juvenile officers who are specialists in dealing with youths. The right kind of police can do much to alleviate youthful crime in their communities, yet without incarceration and harsh punishment. Some police organize boys clubs, offer drug education programs, talk to youth groups and do much of a positive nature to prevent juvenile crime.

The Juvenile Court

As a last resort, the juvenile court is asked to make the disposition of a case. But cases are often dealt with informally in private hearings in the judge's chambers, without any formal trial. What happens in such cases depends completely on the inclinations of the judge. Plea bargaining is common, so that the attorneys decide the case.

At the present time, the best juvenile court systems hire judges with special qualifications for juvenile court work, judges who understand not only the law but child psychology and social problems as well. A variety of medical, psychological, psychosomatic, and social services are available along with adequate foster family and institutional care, as well as recreational services and facilities. A qualified probation staff plans constructive programs under state supervision. Detention of juveniles is kept at a minimum.

The Correctional System

The majority of juvenile offenders brought to court, especially those charged with a first offense, are placed on probation, given suspended sentences, and ordered to get help from the proper medical or psychological personnel or social service agency. The whole purpose of the court is not to punish, but to try to rehabilitate the delinquent. Thus, the judge most often makes quick decisions regarding the best treatment.

The backbone of the correctional procedure is the probation system, whereby the juvenile is placed under the care of a probation officer to whom the juvenile must report and who strives to regulate and guide his or her conduct. Probation that is based entirely on the threat of punishment is poor rehabilitation. Programs that focus on positive behavior and positive reinforcement are more helpful. Studies show that juvenile offenders placed on probation have lower rearrest rates and generally better overall records than those detained in juvenile facilities.

Most juvenile correction systems include detention centers of one kind or another. Most of these are reception and diagnostic centers where juveniles are placed under temporary restraint awaiting a hearing. If a hearing has already been held, a youth may be placed in such a center for further diagnosis and evaluation before more permanent action is taken. About one fourth of the youths in detention centers are not even delinquents; they are usually wards of the state whose parents can't or won't care for them. These young people may be placed alongside sexual psychopaths or narcotics peddlers so that, as any youth who has been there can tell you, juvenile centers are no place for juveniles.

The correctional system also includes training schools, ranches, forestry camps, and farms. About three fourths of the juveniles held in public custody are placed in these types of facilities. Most authorities feel that such training schools and correctional institutions do not correct or rehabilitate. While youths are being punished, "rehabilitated," or "corrected," they are exposed to hundreds of other delinquents who spend their time running their own behavior modification program to shape additional antisocial and delinquent behavior. The influence is therefore quite negative. The system has been improved greatly by what has been called the *token economy,* which places the emphasis on a "24-hour positive learning environment." In this system, students earn points for good behavior, with points convertible to money that can be used to purchase goods or privileges. Students earn points for doing chores, for academic accomplishments and school work, for proper social behavior, or for social development. Under this system, youths make great gains in academic achievement, on-the-job training, or in eliminating assaultive, disruptive, and antisocial behavior.

Sending adolescents to prison is the worst way to rehabilitate them. An advertisement for the National Council on Crime and Delinquency in *Time* magazine, June 15, 1970, shows a boy with a gun in his hand and the caption reads: "Prison isn't a waste of time, a lot of kids come out learning a trade" (Goshen, 1971). Goshen estimates that only 10 to 20 percent of a prison population are "sociopaths" who prefer antisocial behavior, who have no regard for the interests of others, who show little or no remorse, who are untreatable, and for whom prison may be justified. The remainder only learn to be hardened criminals while in prison, since they are often mistreated by guards or harassed and bullied by fellow prisoners. If adolescents are not antagonistic toward authority and the system upon arrival in prison, they soon acquire that attitude. They grow to hate the prison and vow never to return, not by becoming law-abiding, but by never again being caught. Prison provides a model of criminal behavior; it unleashes on prisoners the revenge of society, guards, and other prisoners; and it stimulates each inmate to want to get out to seek his or her own vengeance.

Private, Community Programs

Private, community programs established to treat delinquency have taken many forms. Communities have established drug abuse centers, rap centers, coffee houses, youth centers, boys or girls clubs, big brother or big sister programs, and youth employment agencies.

MORAL TEACHINGS

There are several things that parents should try to teach from the time their children are little.

Property

One is respect for the property of others. Preschoolers will often take crayons or other small items home from nursery school or kindergarten, without realizing that it is wrong. Such items should be returned, and children taught that they are not to help themselves to things that don't belong to them. The late preschool and early grade school years are the appropriate times to teach the commandment "You shall not steal" (Ex. 20:15).

If children are caught stealing, the parents should make every effort to get at the reasons. One boy I know would steal and then hide the objects under his pillow, where his mother found them while making the bed. The mother would report the theft to the father, and he would spank the boy. When I asked the boy why he stole and then put the things under his pillow where they would be found, he replied: "I know they'll find them, and give me a spanking. But when I don't steal, they never pay any attention to me." He would rather have a spanking and be noticed, than to be rejected and neglected! In such cases, the parents probably need counseling help to straighten out the situation.

Teenagers often become involved in petty crimes such as shoplifting. They do it for various reasons: because their friends do, or because their friends pressure them to do so; because they haven't any money and feel they need something badly enough to steal it; as an expression of deep-seated problems of hostility, resentment, or rebellion; or just for kicks, because they think it's fun trying to outwit the storekeeper or police. Some steal so they can sell the goods to get money for drugs. Others steal because of poor moral training, and lack of impulse control. Such petty crimes can be serious, so parents should make every effort to correct the behavior. Certainly they should not overlook even the pettiest of crimes, but make their children return the objects, and make restitution, primarily through work and money payments.

Honesty

Various surveys report that more than 90 percent of high school students admit to having cheated in school at various times (Thornburg, 1975, p. 188). Some students will give others help on tests, but will not ask for illegal help themselves. More boys than girls report taking illegal notes or aids into examinations, turning in work done by others (such as parents), plagiarizing material, removing books from the library illegally, forging teachers' or parents' names, lying about school to parents, feigning illness in order to skip school, failing to turn in valuables that have been found, or giving other students higher grades than they deserve in correcting papers (Thornburg, 1975, p. 189). Thus, boys seem more willing than girls to accept the idea of general dishonesty within the school. This finding is in keeping with the fact that girls are usually more conforming in their behavior than are boys. Boys often show more rebellion and a willingness to adopt antisocial behavior.

When asked why they cheat, students report fear of failure as the main cause, lack of study because of laziness, need to satisfy parental demands, need to make good grades to get into college, the difficulty of school work, or the ease with which cheating can be accomplished (Thornburg, 1975, p. 189).

Teachers and parents need to be more open in discussing problems of cheating, and to make greater efforts to teach basic honesty. Sometimes the issues are never discussed with teachers or parents. I know that colleges with an honor system spend a great deal of time and effort indoctrinating entering freshmen on the importance of honesty in exam-taking, and on the need for all to make the honor system work. If definite policies are established, and repeated efforts are made to teach the importance of honesty, students are more likely to conform to this social pressure to be honest.

Truthfulness

The same principles hold true in teaching children the importance of telling the truth, and in not telling lies. If they have been thoroughly indoctrinated in these principles from the time they are young, if parents set a good example themselves, and if they make every effort to guide their children and to discipline them when they tell falsehoods, by the time the children reach adolescence they are more likely to have well-established habits of truthfulness that they carry with them into adulthood. "You shall not bear false witness against your neighbor" (Ex. 20:16) is as important today to all trusting human relationships as it was when it was written.

References

Achtemeier, E. *The Committed Marriage.* Westminster Press, 1976.

Adelson, J. "The Political Imagination of the Young Adolescent." In Kagan, J., and Coles, R. (eds.), *Twelve to Sixteen: Early Adolescence.* W. W. Norton & Co., 1972.

Albrecht, S. L., et al. "Religiosity and Deviance: Application of an Attitude-Behavior Contingent Consistency Model." *Journal for the Scientific Study of Religion* 16 (Sept. 1977): 263–274.

Alexander, R. G. "Can a Christian Ethic Condone Behavior Modification?" *Religion in Life* 45 (Summer 1976): 191–203.

Allport, G. W. "Values and Our Youth." *Teachers College Record* 63 (1961): 211–219.

Babin, P. "The Faith of Adolescents Toward the End of School." *Religious Education* 57 (1962): 128–131.

—— *Adolescents in Search of a New Church,* tr. and adapted by Nancy Hennessy and Carol White. Herder & Herder, 1970.

Bachman, J. G., and Johnston, L. D. "The Freshmen, 1979." *Psychology Today,* Sept. 1979, pp. 79ff.

Bacon, M.K., and Jones, M.B. *Teen-Age Drinking.* Thomas Y. Crowell Co., 1968

Bainton, R. H. *What Christianity Says About Sex, Love and Marriage.* Association Press, 1957.

Bandura, A. *Aggression: A Social Learning Analysis.* Prentice-Hall, 1973.

Bandura, A., and Perloff, B. "Relative Efficacy of Self-Monitored and Externally Imposed Reinforcement Systems." *Journal of*

Personality and Social Psychology 7 (1967): 11–116.

Bandura, A.; Ross, D.; and Ross, S. A. "Invitation of Film-Mediated Aggressive Models." *Journal of Abnormal and Social Psychology* 66 (1963): 3–11.

Bandura, A., and Walters, R. H. *Adolescent Aggression.* Ronald Press Co., 1959.

—————— *Social Learning and Personality Development.* Holt, Rinehart & Winston, 1963.

Barnes, C. W. National Education Association. *Journal of Proceedings and Addresses.* Winona, Minn.: NEA, 1911.

Bender, S. J. "Sex and the College Student." *Journal of School Health* 43 (May 1973): 278–280.

Bert-Hallahmi, B. "Self-Reported Religious Concerns of University Underclassmen." *Adolescence* 9 (1974): 333–338.

The Book of Common Worship. Board of Christian Education, the Presbyterian Church U.S.A., 1946.

Bowlby, J. *Child Care and the Growth of Love.* Pelican Books, 1965.

Brill, M. L., et al. (eds.). *Write Your Own Wedding.* Association Press, 1973.

Bronfenbrenner, U. *Two Worlds of Childhood: U.S. and U.S.S.R.* Russell Sage Foundation, 1970.

Burns, J. A. *The Catholic School System in the United States: Its Principles, Origin and Establishment.* Benziger Brothers, 1908.

Bushnell, H. "Christianity and Common Schools." *Common School Journal of Connecticut* 11 (Jan. 15, 1840): 102.

Cater, D., and Strickland, S. *TV Violence and the Child.* Russell Sage Foundation, 1975.

Catholic Theological Society of America, Committee on the Study of Human Sexuality. *Human Sexuality: New Directions in American Catholic Thought.* Paulist Press, 1977.

Chilton, R. J., and Markle, G. E. "Family Disruption, Delinquent Conduct, and the Effect of Subclassification." *American Sociological Review* 37 (1972): 93–99.

Cole, W. G. *Sex and Love in the Bible.* Association Press, 1959.

Committee on Character Education. "Preliminary Report." In National Education Association, *Proceedings.* Washington, D.C.: NEA, 1924, pp. 278–279.

Costanzo, P. R., and Shaw, M. E. "Conformity as a Function of

Age Level." *Child Development* 37 (1966): 967–975.

Culley, J. D., et al. "The Experts Look at Children's Television." *Journal of Broadcasting* 20 (Winter 1976): 3–21.

Cully, K. B. (ed.). *The Westminster Dictionary of Christian Education.* Westminster Press, 1963.

Curtis, D. "The Re-making of a Revolutionary." *Student Action* 5 (1971): 2, 7.

Dewey, J. *Moral Principles in Education.* (1909 edition.) Reprint, Southern Illinois Press, 1975.

——— "Character." In P. Monroe (ed.), *Cyclopedia of Education.* The Macmillan Co., 1911.

Dickinson, G. E. "Religious Practices of Adolescents in a Southern Community: 1964–1974." *Journal for the Scientific Study of Religion* 15 (Dec. 1976): 361–363.

Donohue, T. R. "Black Children's Perceptions of Favorite TV Characters as Models of Antisocial Behavior." *Journal of Broadcasting* 19 (Spring 1975): 153–167.

——— "Favorite TV Characters as Behavioral Models for the Emotionally Disturbed." *Journal of Broadcasting* 21 (Summer 1977): 333–345.

Donovan, F. R. *Wild Kids.* Stackpole Co., 1967.

Donovan, J. M. "Identity Status and Interpersonal Style." *Journal of Youth and Adolescence* 4 (1975): 37–55.

Elder, C. A. *Values and Moral Development in Children.* Broadman Press, 1976.

Elkind, D. "Egocentrism in Adolescence." *Child Development* 38 (1967): 1025–1034.

Engel, D. E. "Education and Identity: The Functions of Questions in Religious Education." *Religious Education* 63 (1968): 371–375.

Engel v. *Vitale,* 8 L. ed. 2d 601, 604 (1962).

English, O. S., and Pearson, G. H. J. *Emotional Problems of Living.* W. W. Norton & Co., 1945.

Eppel, E. M., and Eppel, M. *Adolescents and Morality.* Humanities Press, 1966.

Ferguson, C. *Organizing to Beat the Devil: Methodists and the Making of America.* Doubleday & Co., 1971.

Fletcher, J. *Situation Ethics: The New Morality.* Westminster Press, 1966.

Floyd, H. H., Jr., and South, D. R. "Dilemma of Youth: The

Choice of Parents or Peers as a Frame of Reference for Behavior." *Journal of Marriage and the Family* 34 (1972): 627–634.

Forisha, B. E., and Forisha, B. E. *Moral Development and Education.* Lincoln, Neb.: Professional Educators Publications, 1976.

Forrest, J. D., et al. "Abortion in the United States, 1976–1977." *Family Planning Perspectives* 10 (Sept.–Oct. 1978): 271–279.

Fraenkel, J. R. *How to Teach About Values: An Analytic Approach.* Prentice-Hall, 1977.

Freud, S. *New Introductory Lectures on Psycho-analysis,* tr. by W. J. H. Sprott. W. W. Norton & Co., 1933.

Friedman, C. J., et al. "Juvenile Street Gangs: The Victimization of Youth." *Adolescence* 11 (1976): 527–533.

Gannon, T. M. "Religious Control and Delinquent Behavior." *Sociology and Social Research* 51 (1967): 418–431.

Goshen, C. E. "The Characterology of Adolescent Offenders and the Management of Prisons." *Adolescence* 6 (1971): 167–186.

Greenberg, B. S., and Dervin, B. (eds.). *Use of the Mass Media by the Urban Poor.* Frederick A. Praeger, 1970.

Gunter, B. G., and Moore, H. A. "Youth, Leisure, and Post-Industrial Society: Implications for the Family." *The Family Life Coordinator* 24 (1975): 199–207.

Hall, B. P. *Value Clarification as Learning Process: A Guidebook.* Paulist Press, 1973.

Hall, R. T. "Morality and Religion in Public Education: A Dialogue." *Religious Education* 72 (May–June 1977): 273–292.

Hall, R. T., and Davis, J. U. *Moral Education in Theory and Practice.* Prometheus Books, 1975.

Hanson, R. F., and Carlson, R. E. *Organizations for Children and Youth.* Prentice-Hall, 1972.

Harlow, H. F. "The Nature of Love." *American Psychologist* 13 (1958): 673–685.

——— "The Heterosexual Affectional System in Monkeys." *American Psychologist* 17 (1962): 1–9.

Harlow, H. F., and Suomi, S. J. "The Nature of Love—Simplified." *American Psychologist* 25 (1970): 161–168.

Harris, A. *Teaching Morality and Religion.* London: George Allen & Unwin, 1976.

Hastings, P. K., and Hoge, D. R. "Changes in Religion Among College Students, 1948 to 1974." *Journal for the Scientific Study of Religion* 15 (Sept. 1976): 237–249.

Hilts, P. J. *Behavior Modification.* Harper's Magazine Press, 1974, pp. 41, 42.

Horn, D., et al. "Cigarette Smoking Among High School Students." *American Journal of Public Health* 49 (1959): 1497–1511.

"How Much Does He Do Around the House?" *Changing Times* 25 (April 1971): 41.

Howell, M. "Employed Mothers and Their Families: Part I." *Pediatrics* 52 (Aug. 1973): 256.

Humphrey, F. G. As reported in: "Study Says Adultery Is Serious Problem." *Portland Press Herald* (Portland, Me.), April 11, 1977.

Illinois ex. rel. *McCollum* v. *Board of Education,* 68 S. ct. 461 at 477 (1948).

Jacobsen, R. B., et al. "An Empirical Test of the Generation Gap: A Comparative Intrafamily Study." *Journal of Marriage and Family* 37 (1975): 841–852.

Jones, V. "Attitudes of College Students and Their Changes: A 37-Year Study." *Journal of Genetic Psychology* 3 (1970): 80.

Kee, H. C. *Making Ethical Decisions.* Westminster Press, 1957.

King, M. L. *Why We Can't Wait.* Harper & Row, 1964.

Kirschenbaum, H. *Advanced Value Clarification.* University Associates, 1977.

Kohlberg, L. "Moral Education in the Schools: A Developmental View." *The School Review* 74 (1966): 1–30.

——— *Stages in the Development of Moral Thought and Action.* Holt, Rinehart & Winston, 1969.

Lannie, V. P. "The Teaching of Values in Public, Sunday and Catholic Schools: An Historical Perspective." *Religious Education* 70 (March-April 1975): 115–137.

Lehmann, P. L. *Ethics in a Christian Context.* Harper & Row, 1963.

LeMasters, E. E. *Parents in Modern America.* Rev. ed. Dorsey Press, 1974.

Lerman, P. "Individual Values, Peer Values, and Subcultural Delinquency." *American Sociological Review* 33 (1968): 219–235.

Lewis, S. *First Annual Report of the Superintendent of Common Schools.* Columbus, Ohio, 1838.

Liebert, R. M., et al. *The Early Window: Effects of Television on*

Children and Youth. Pergamon Press, 1973.

Liebert, R. M., and Neale, J. M. "TV Violence and Child Aggression: Snow on the Screen." *Psychology Today* 5 (1972): 38–40.

Looney, G. "The Ecology of Childhood." In E. Sarson (ed.), *Action for Children's Television.* Avon Books, 1971.

Magnuson, W., Senator. "Television Violence." *Congressional Record,* Vol. 121, No. 188 (Dec. 18, 1975).

Mantz, B. "What Are Your Children Being Taught About Morality?" *Better Homes and Gardens,* Sept. 1978, pp. 16ff.

Maslow, A. H. *Toward a Psychology of Being.* Van Nostrand Reinhold Co., 1968.

McCluskey, N. G. *Public Schools and Moral Education.* Columbia University Press, 1958.

Murray, J. O. *A Popular History of the Catholic Church in the United States.* New York, 1876.

Nye, F. I. *Family Relationships and Delinquent Behavior.* John Wiley & Sons, 1958.

Oates, W. E. *On Becoming Children of God.* Westminster Press, 1969.

Pagliuso, S. *Understanding Stages of Moral Development: A Programmed Learning Workbook.* Paulist Press, 1976.

Pastore, J., Senator. "Family Viewing—A Responsible Answer to the Problem of Televised Violence." *Congressional Record,* Vol. 121, No. 188 (Dec. 18, 1975).

Peters, R. S. "Moral Development and Moral Learning." *The Monist* 58 (Oct. 1974): 541–567.

Piaget, J. *The Moral Judgment of the Child.* Tr. by Marjorie Gabain Free Press, 1948.

———— *Six Psychological Studies.* Tr. by A. Tenzer and D. Elkind. Random House, 1967.

Pomeroy, D. W. "The New Nihilism." *Theology Today* 31 (Oct. 1974): 248–257.

Ramsdell, M. L. "The Trauma of TV's Troubled Soap Families." *The Family Life Coordinator* 22 (1973): 299–304.

Raths, L. E.; Harmin, M.; and Simon, S. B. *Values and Teaching.* Charles E. Merrill Publishing Co., 1966; 2d ed. 1978.

Rice, F. P. *The Adolescent: Development, Relationships, and Culture.* 2d ed. Allyn & Bacon, 1978.

———— *Sexual Problems in Marriage: Help from a Christian Counselor.* Westminster Press, 1978a.

———— *Marriage and Parenthood.* Allyn & Bacon, 1979.

———— *The Working Mother's Guide to Child Development.* Prentice-Hall, 1979.

Robins, L. N. *Deviant Children Grown Up.* Williams & Wilkins Co., 1966.

Roper Organization. "Sex . . . Marriage . . . Divorce—What Women Think Today." *U.S. News & World Report* 77 (Oct. 21, 1974): 107.

Rosen, B. C. *Adolescence and Religion.* Schenkman Publishing Co., 1965.

Rosenhan, D. "Some Origins of Concern for Others." In P. Mussen; J. Langer; and M. Covington (eds.), *Trends and Issues in Developmental Psychology.* Holt, Rinehart & Winston, 1969.

Rubin, A. M. "Television Usage, Attitudes and Viewing Behaviors of Children and Adolescents." *Journal of Broadcasting* 21 (Summer 1977): 355–369.

Schwartz, M., and Tangri, S. S. "A Note on Self-Concept as an Insulator Against Delinquency." *American Sociological Review,* 30 (1965): 922–934.

Simon, S. B., et al. *Values Clarification: A Handbook of Practical Strategies for Teachers and Students.* Hart Publishing Co., 1972.

Skinner, B. F. *Beyond Freedom and Dignity.* Alfred A. Knopf, 1971.

———— *About Behaviorism.* Alfred A. Knopf, 1974.

Sontag, F. "The New Moon Sophistry." *Religion in Life* 46 (Autumn 1977): 269–277.

Stone, L. J., and Church, J. *Childhood and Adolescence: A Psychology of the Growing Person.* Random House, 1958.

Sullivan, E. V. *Moral Learning: Some Findings, Issues and Questions.* Paulist Press, 1975.

Swift, P. "High School Drunks." *Parade Magazine,* Feb. 9, 1975, p. 13.

Taylor, M. (ed.). *Progress and Problems in Moral Education.* Windsor, Berks, England: N.F.E.R. Publishing Co., 1975.

Tec, N. "Family and Differential Involvement with Marihuana: A Study of Suburban Teenagers." *Journal of Marriage and the Family* 32 (1970): 656–664.

———— "Parent-Child Drug Abuse: Generational Continuity or

Adolescent Deviancy." *Adolescence* 9 (1974): 351–364.

"TV Study Shows Violence High Saturday AM's." *Portland Press Herald* (Portland, Me.), Feb. 17, 1977.

Thornburg, H. D. *Development in Adolescence.* Brooks/Cole Publishing Co., 1975.

U.S. Department of Commerce, Bureau of the Census. *Statistical Abstract of the U.S., 1976.* Washington, D.C.: U.S. Government Printing Office, 1976.

U.S. Department of Health, Education, and Welfare. Public Health Service. *Alcohol and Health.* Second Report to the U.S. Congress, 1974. Rockville, Md.: National Institute on Alcohol Abuse and Alcoholism, 1975.

U.S. Surgeon General. Advisory Committee on Television and Children's Aggression. *Television and Growing Up: The Impact of Televised Violence.* Washington, D.C.: U.S. Government Printing Office, Jan. 17, 1972.

Vincent, J. H. *Little Footprints in Bible Lands; or, Simple Lessons in Sacred History and Geography; For the Use of Palestine Classes and Sabbath Schools.* New York, 1861.

—— *Sunday School Institutes and Normal Classes.* New York, 1872.

—— *The Chautauqua Movement.* Boston, 1886.

—— *The Modern Sunday School.* New York, 1887.

Westoff, L. A. "Kids with Kids." *New York Times Magazine,* Feb. 22, 1976, p. 24.

Wilson, J. *Moral Thinking.* London: Heinemann Educational Books, 1970.

—— *Practical Methods of Moral Education.* London: Heinemann Educational Books, 1972.

Wogaman, J. P. *A Christian Method of Moral Judgment.* Westminster Press, 1976.

Yankelovich, D. *The New Morality: A Profile of American Youth in the Seventies.* McGraw-Hill Book Co., 1974.

Zelnik, M., et al. "Probabilities of Intercourse and Conception Among U.S. Teenage Women 1971 and 1976." *Family Planning Perspectives* 11 (May/June 1979): 177–183.

—— and Kantner, J. F. "Contraceptive Patterns and Premarital Pregnancy Among Women Ages 15–19 in 1976." *Family Planning Perspectives* 10 (May/June 1978): 135–142.

Zorach v. *Clauson,* 343 U.S. at 314 (1952).